TOWARDS A EUROPEAN PUBLIC LAW

Pour Peter et Suzanne Richards,
avec mes pensées de fidèle
amitié - and all the best,

B Stirn

le 6.V.2013

Towards a European Public Law

BERNARD STIRN

Translated and edited by

EIRIK BJORGE

OXFORD
UNIVERSITY PRESS

OXFORD

UNIVERSITY PRESS

Great Clarendon Street, Oxford, OX2 6DP,
United Kingdom

Oxford University Press is a department of the University of Oxford.
It furthers the University's objective of excellence in research, scholarship,
and education by publishing worldwide. Oxford is a registered trade mark of
Oxford University Press in the UK and in certain other countries

First Edition published in 2017

Impression: 1

Published in the United States of America by Oxford University Press
198 Madison Avenue, New York, NY 10016, United States of America

British Library Cataloguing in Publication Data
Data available

Library of Congress Control Number: 2017931338

ISBN 978-0-19-878950-5

Printed and bound by
CPI Group (UK) Ltd, Croydon, CR0 4YY

The genius of Vienna, a specifically musical genius, had always been that it harmonised all national and linguistic opposites in itself; its culture was a synthesis of all Western cultures. Anyone who lived and worked there felt free of narrow-minded prejudice. Nowhere was it easier to be a European.

—Stefan Zweig, *The World of Yesterday* (1943)

Foreword

In his *Introduction to the Law of the Constitution,* first published in 1885, the English constitutional scholar A V Dicey described French *droit administratif* as utterly unlike any branch of modern English law: even the term, he wrote, had no proper equivalent in English legal phraseology. That view was greatly exaggerated: Dicey appears to have misunderstood the French system of administrative law, and to have overlooked the existence of a substantial body of English law on the same subject. In fairness, he later came to adopt a more nuanced view. His earlier writings were, however, highly influential in forming British attitudes towards continental systems of public law. And some significant differences did exist. Whereas administrative law became increasingly important in France and Germany as the activities of the state developed during the first half of the twentieth century, and a constant stream of judgments was analysed and systematized by legal scholars, there was, for quite a prolonged period, comparatively little activity in that area of the law in the United Kingdom. Furthermore, the establishment of judicial institutions to apply administrative law which were wholly separate from the ordinary courts, such as the French Conseil d'État, had no parallel in the United Kingdom. Even the concept of the state had no equivalent in English law, and no clear distinction was drawn between private and public law.

These differences between Britain and continental Europe had deep roots. Constitutional developments in seventeenth century England, themselves with roots in a more distant past, had prevented the Crown from establishing a degree of control over the country equivalent to that exercised from Versailles or Potsdam. The range of functions performed by government remained comparatively limited until modern times, and government departments were surprisingly small. The absence of any rupture with constitutional tradition, equivalent to that resulting from the revolutions of French and German history, allowed the law to evolve incrementally, without any fundamental re-consideration of its approach to the exercise of public functions, or of the institutions responsible for the administration of justice in that field.

The second half of the twentieth century witnessed major changes, as the law in the United Kingdom responded to the growth of the state and the expansion of its functions. A renaissance of administrative law began in the 1960s, building on the older body of case law. Remedies in public law became more readily available, with the introduction in the 1970s of the application for judicial review. New institutional arrangements were established, with the creation of numerous administrative tribunals and, eventually, their closer integration into the framework and culture of the courts and the judiciary.

But the most significant changes in this area of the law, influencing those already discussed but having a broader impact, have occurred over the last forty years or so as a result of the UK's membership of the European Union and its adherence to the European Convention on Human Rights and Fundamental Freedoms, as given domestic effect by the Human Rights Act 1998. These changes have also affected, to a greater or lesser degree, the other European countries that belong to the European Union and adhere to the European Convention, and have resulted in a growing convergence of some aspects of the different European legal traditions. Although the differences between those traditions in some respects remain profound, they have diminished considerably in the field of public law.

The European Union is based on law: not only in the formal sense that it has been established by international treaties entered into by the Member States, but also in the more fundamental sense that it is a system founded on law, in which the courts play a central role in supervising legislative and governmental institutions, and in which the Court of Justice ensures the consistent interpretation of EU law by the national courts by means of the preliminary reference procedure. In exercising its interpretative function, the Court of Justice has consciously furthered the goal of integration by adopting a robustly purposive approach, and the national courts have then become the agents of integration by giving effect to that purposive interpretation. There is, however, scope for dialogue between the Court of Justice and national courts, both literally in meetings between their respective judges, and more figuratively in their respective judgments.

The European Convention is also an international treaty, whose interpretation is the task of another international court—the European Court of Human Rights. National courts in turn generally give effect to its interpretation of the Convention, at least when it has become the settled view. The scope for dialogue in this context is more firmly established: through their respective judgments, national courts such as the Supreme Court of the United Kingdom, and the European Court of Human Rights, can conduct a prolonged and fruitful dialogue. The scope for national courts to influence the European Court is widened by the Court's doctrine of the national margin of appreciation, which enables it, within limits, to respect national differences and sensitivities.

These developments have challenged some older attitudes to the role of the courts in public affairs in the United Kingdom. The European Union is a system in which the courts play a more prominent role than was traditional in this country. As the ambit of EU law has progressively widened, so as to cover not only matters directly relating to trade, but also broader and more sensitive issues, such as immigration, data protection, and the environment, an increasing range of aspects of public administration have become subject to EU law, and therefore to adjudication by the courts. At the same time, the European Convention has required domestic courts to make judgments on an even wider range of issues, sometimes relating to controversial issues of social or economic policy.

Both the establishment of the European Union and the task of interpreting and applying the European Convention have depended on recognizing, and building on, the fundamental values which the different national legal cultures have in common: values with their roots in a shared European cultural tradition. They include the values that find expression in the concepts of the rule of law, the *Rechtsstaat*, and the *État de droit*, such as the independence of the judiciary, the right of access to a court, and the right to a fair trial, and the other values which are reflected in the guarantees contained in the EU Charter of Fundamental Rights and the European Convention. These shared values also include basic constitutional principles, such as the separation of powers between the courts and the other institutions of government. At the same time, the application of both EU law and the European Convention has also given rise to constitutional problems which are common to many of the Member States: for example, as to the relationship between the legal order established by the EU treaties and national constitutional principles, and as to how, in concrete situations, the separation of powers between the courts and the elected branches of government should be demarcated.

In addition to fundamental values held in common, and a shared understanding of the broad elements of constitutionalism, the successful application of EU law and the European Convention also requires the application by the national courts of shared general principles of administrative law. Fortunately, the Court of Justice and the European Court of Human Rights have established common principles, derived principally from French and German administrative law, such as legal certainty, the protection of legitimate expectations, equality, non-discrimination, proportionality, and subsidiarity. Their application has become a familiar aspect of the work of national courts, even in countries such as the United Kingdom, where different principles were formerly applied (and continue to be applied outside the European context). Cultural adaptation to these principles, and understanding their relationship to the apparently different principles established in domestic administrative law, has been another challenge. Some principles, such as the protection of legitimate expectations, have been absorbed into the domestic administrative law of the United Kingdom. The absorption of others, such as proportionality, remains controversial. Some judges and academic commentators have come to feel that the differences between proportionality and reasonableness are more apparent than real: a matter of articulating explicitly an analysis which is in any event implicit. Others think that there are real differences affecting the separation of powers.

As the ambit of EU law has widened over time, and as the influence of the European Convention on the national law of many countries, including the United Kingdom, has developed, these general principles have become increasingly central to the application of public law in all the Member States. That is one factor which has drawn the courts of the Member States closer together. But more generally, because EU law and the European Convention give rise to legal issues which affect the courts of the Member States in common, the process of European integration has been accompanied by a considerable increase in the frequency and intensity of discussions between the leading courts in those countries. Dialogues involving, for example, the Supreme Court of the United Kingdom, the French Conseil d'État and Conseil constitutionnel, the German Federal Constitutional Court, and the Italian Consiglio di Stato have become well established. Through these dialogues, United Kingdom courts, and their counterparts in other jurisdictions, have learned from each other's experience and jurisprudence. These dialogues between national courts have been accompanied by the establishment of parallel dialogues between each of those courts and the European Court of Human Rights, conducted partly through meetings but also through their judgments. Although less fully developed, a third dialogue has also been initiated between the Court of Justice and national courts.

These developments—the central role of courts in the development of the European Union and in the application of the European Convention; the development of European law on the basis of fundamental values held in common, shared constitutional values, and common principles of public law; and the development of judicial dialogue both at the national level and between the national courts and the European courts—lie at the heart of the present work, which was originally published in French as *Vers un droit public européen* (the first edition in 2012, and the second in 2015), and has been ably translated for this English edition by Dr Eirik Bjorge, senior lecturer in Law at the University of Bristol.

The author, Bernard Stirn, has been President of the Section du contentieux (the Judicial Section) of the Conseil d'État since 2006, and is one of Europe's most senior and respected judges in the field of public law, as well as being a distinguished university teacher. He is very well placed to describe the developments that have taken place and to analyse their implications.

His central theme is that a European public law is being created by three interlocking mechanisms: the development of the European Union, the jurisprudence of the European Court of Human Rights, and the domestic laws of the nations of Europe. These three sources of law influence each other through the interactions of the Court of Justice of the European Union, the European Court of Human Rights, and the national constitutional courts and other apex courts. Their interactions result in the creation of a body of European public law, founded on common values with deep roots in European history.

So, after a lucid and succinct account of the phases of European integration since the Second World War, through the European Union, the Council of Europe, and other European institutions, the author provides in the succeeding chapters an account of the European legal order at the present day, and the relationship between European and domestic law. He then turns to institutional arrangements, considering first the independence of the judiciary and the dialogue between judges, and then turning to the development of a European model of public administration. Finally, he turns to the future, and the challenges facing European law.

The book can be recommended to students and the wider public as a masterly and authoritative guide to European institutions and the European movement, and a stimulating discussion of recent legal developments. It can also be recommended to those lawyers and judges who are interested in standing back from their daily routine and considering what has been happening to public law in Europe over the past few decades, and where it might be heading.

This English edition appears at a time when the UK's future relationship with the rest of Europe is unclear. It is impossible at present to predict what changes to our law may result from withdrawal from the European Union. Equally, although the Government has spoken of replacing the Human Rights Act with a domestic Bill of Rights, the nature of any Bill of Rights, its timing, and whether the United Kingdom will remain a party to the European Convention remain to be seen. Nevertheless, the United Kingdom will continue to share with other European nations a cultural heritage, and many of our legal concepts and principles. European influence on the law of the UK's jurisdictions did not begin with our entry into the European Union, and is unlikely to end with our withdrawal. The opening lines of T S Eliot's *Burnt Norton* may be apposite:

Time present and time past,
Are both perhaps present in time future,
And time future contained in time past.

The Rt Hon Lord Reed
15 March 2017

Preface

Vers un droit public européen has been published in two editions in French, in 2012 and 2015.[1] This English version is a translation of the 2015 edition, made before the referendum on 23 June 2016 on Brexit. It thus does not take into account the consequences—still incidentally difficult to determine—of that referendum.

Whatever the outcome of the procedure of extrication opened up by that referendum, the analyses contained in this book of the emergence of a European public law—on the basis of the law of the European Union,[2] the law of the European Convention on Human Rights,[3] and that of the domestic law of the European countries— retain their importance and topicality. The co-existence of the different sources of law leads, in all Europe, to important consequences as regards the hierarchy of norms, the role of the courts, and the equilibrium of the legal system.

These effects are, of course, more pronounced for those countries which belong both to the European Union and to the Council of Europe. But, even if the United Kingdom does leave the European Union, it will remain a member of the Council of Europe and maintain specific relations with the European Union. The country and its legal system will, consequently, remain affected by the force and developments of European law.

Bernard Stirn
Paris
20 August 2016

---

[1] B Stirn, *Vers un droit public européen* (2nd edn, LGDJ 2015).

[2] Consolidated versions of the treaty on European Union and the Treaty on the Functioning of the European Union [2016] OJ C202; Charter of Fundamental Rights of the European Union [2016] OJ C202.

[3] Convention for the Protection of Human Rights and Fundamental Freedoms, 4 November 1950, 213 UNTS 221.

Summary Contents

Contents

Table of Cases

Tables of Legislation

EU LEGISLATION

Regulations

Directives

OTHER JURISDICTIONS

France

Germany

Greece

Italy

Poland

Portugal

Soviet Union

1

Introduction

> What, then, is Europe? It is a kind of cape of the old continent, a
> western appendix to Asia. It looks naturally to the west. On the
> south it is bordered by a famous sea whose role, or should I say
> function, has been wonderfully effective in the development of
> that European spirit with which we are concerned.
>
> —Paul Valéry, *The European* (1924)

Europa, an elusive mythological figure carried across the sea by Zeus,
gave her name to a continent in mysterious circumstances. In the
fifth century BCE, while his contemporary Pericles was consolidating
Athenian democracy, Herodotus wrote: 'it is clear that Europa was of
Asiatic birth, and never came to the land that the Greeks now call Europe,
but only from Phoenicia to Crete and from Crete to Lycia.'[1] Since then,
however, through geography, and even more importantly, through history, art, and culture, a distinctive European identity has evolved. Born
in Athens, the epitome of the city-states of ancient Greece, the theory
of a democratic constitution was first articulated in the writings of the
philosophers Plato and Aristotle. The Roman Empire, which covered
much of Europe, survived in the West as the Empire of Charlemagne
(who was given the title *Pater Europae*) and in the East as the Empire
of Byzantium. The kingdom of the Plantagenets straddled France and
England. 'One could continue to dream, on both sides of the Channel',

---

[1] Herodotus, *Histories* 4.45.5.

Towards a European Public Law. First Edition. Bernard Stirn. © Bernard Stirn 2017.
Published 2017 by Oxford University Press.

wrote the French historian Jean Favier, 'of what Europe might have been had the fortunes of the Plantagenets persisted'.[2]

The Renaissance of the fifteenth and sixteenth centuries, the Enlightenment of the eighteenth, and the Romanticism of the nineteenth century were movements common to all of Europe. Artists, writers, painters, and musicians made their contribution to the development of a European culture, expressing themselves according to the diverse genius of their nations. 'Dante, Goethe, and Chateaubriand belong to all of Europe to the very extent that they were respectively and eminently Italian, German, and French', wrote de Gaulle.[3] Some—such as Erasmus, Leonardo da Vinci, Mozart, Handel, Byron, Liszt, Turgenev, Mann, and Picasso—lived and worked firmly within a European context.

That common cultural heritage had political concomitants. After each of the great European conflicts, an attempt was made through international treaty-making to draw up a framework of stability. At the end of the Thirty Years' War, the principle of the nation state was established by the Treaty of Westphalia (1648).[4] At the Congress of Vienna (1814–15)[5] an equilibrium was sought with a view to drawing the Napoleonic era to a close on the basis of what Talleyrand already called the 'public law of Europe'.[6] In the aftermath of the First World War, a new map of Europe was drawn up by the Treaty of Versailles (1919)[7] and that of Saint-Germain (1919).[8] These dispensations, however, regrettably contained within

---

[2] See J Favier, *Les Plantagenêts: origines et destin d'un empire* (Fayard 2004).

[3] C de Gaulle, *Major Addresses, Statements, and Press Conferences of General Charles de Gaulle, May 19, 1958–January 31, 1964* (French Embassy, Press and Information Division 1964) 175.

[4] There were in fact three bilateral treaties: Spain–Netherlands, 30 January 1648, 1 CTS 1; Sweden–Empire, 14 October 1648, 1 CTS 119; France–Empire, 12 October 1648, 1 CTS 271.

[5] Definitive Treaty of Peace between Austria, Great Britain, Prussia and Russia, and France, 20 November 1815, 65 CTS 251.

[6] See eg A Sorel, 'Talleyrand au Congrès de Vienne' in *Essais d'histoire et de critique* (Plon 1883).

[7] Treaty of Versailles, 28 June 1919, 225 CTS 188.

[8] Treaty between the Allied and Associated Powers and the Kingdom of the Serbs, Croats and Slovenes, 10 September 1919, 226 CTS 186.

them the seeds of the Second World War. As André Gide observed in his diary (26 June 1940):

> We shall always have to pay for the absurdities of the intangible Treaty of Versailles, the humiliations of those once conquered, the useless vexations which turned one's stomach in 1919, but against which it was pointless to protest—the undignified abuse of victory.

Alongside the drama, the divisions, and the rifts, the project of a common European undertaking gradually evolved. 'The day will come when we will see', wrote Victor Hugo in 1849, 'the United States of America and the United States of Europe face to face, reaching out for each other across the seas.' Writing on the heels of the war of 1870, he returned to the idea in a message he sent from Guernsey on 20 September 1872 to the delegates of the Peace Congress gathered at Lugano: 'We will have these great United States of Europe to crown the old world just as the United States of America crown the new one.'

The two World Wars might have put paid forever to ideas of European unity. In *The World of Yesterday*, Stefan Zweig, the *beau idéal* of the pre-war European for whom the continent had no frontiers, described the heartrending experience of the First World War.[9] Having then observed, during the course of the Second World War, the utter abandonment of the values which had given his life meaning, he took his own life in Brazil in 1942. It was, however, on the ruins of Nazi barbarism that the European project found the strength to assert itself. In a speech he gave at Zurich on 19 September 1946, Winston Churchill expounded a prophetic vision of Europe:

> We must build a kind of United States of Europe ... We British have our own Commonwealth of Nations. These do not weaken, on the

---

[9] S Zweig, *The World of Yesterday* (Viking 1943).

contrary they strengthen, the world organisation. They are in fact its main support. And why should there not be a European group which could give a sense of enlarged patriotism and common citizenship to the distracted peoples of this mighty continent? And why should it not take its rightful place with other great groupings and help to shape the honourable destiny of man?

The international context of the Cold War, which had already begun at the end of 1947, accelerated efforts to put in place an organization of Western Europe. From the Council of Europe, created in 1950,[10] and the European Communities (of which the European Coal and Steel Community was based on the 1951 Treaty of Paris,[11] and the European Economic Community and the European Atomic Energy Community on the 1957 Treaty of Rome)[12] Victor Hugo's dream began to become a reality, one that was to a large degree constituted by legal instruments.

Diversity remains key to the legal arrangements of the different countries of Europe, whether at the level of political constitutions, territorial organization, legal systems, or judicial administration. Constitutional monarchies (the United Kingdom, Sweden, Norway, Denmark, Belgium, Luxembourg, and Spain) rub shoulders with republics. Some of the latter are of the parliamentary kind (Germany and Italy); others are presidential (France and Poland). The oldest democracies co-exist with countries that have just shaken from their feet the dust of totalitarianism. State structures vary from the federal model (Germany and Belgium) to the confederative (Switzerland) to the unitary state, with differing degrees of devolved powers. The unwritten constitution of the United Kingdom contrasts with the written ones of other countries; many of the countries have constitutional

---

[10] Statute of the Council of Europe ('Treaty of London'), 5 May 1949, 87 UNTS 103.
[11] Treaty Establishing the European Coal and Steel Community, 18 April 1951, 261 UNTS 140.
[12] Treaty Establishing the European Economic Community, 25 March 1957, 298 UNTS 3.

courts, while others do not. The traditions of Continental law, in turn, contrast with the legal systems of Common Law countries. Certain States maintain a duality of an administrative and an ordinary court structure; others have only one unified judicial structure, as in the United Kingdom.

In the teeth of this heterogeneity, the European project has evolved and been consolidated to a large extent through law. For the European Union (EU) the legal dimension is predominant: it harmonizes legal rules among its members, and defines itself as an integrated legal order. Through the European Convention on Human Rights (ECHR)[13] commonly held principles of law are firmly established. Through their jurisprudence the two European courts—the Court of Justice of the European Union and the European Court of Human Rights—exercise a growing influence on domestic law and on domestic judges.

Against this background, a European public law is taking shape. It is being developed on the basis of three overlapping and mutually reinforcing structures. The first is that of the European Union: for the twenty-eight countries of which it consists, the law of the Union is an influential factor of cohesion as well as an everyday imperative. The second structure is that of the Council of Europe, which ties together the forty-seven countries of Greater Europe that have acceded to it. Bound by the European Convention on Human Rights, they share a set of common obligations in respect of the protection of human rights and fundamental freedoms. But European law does not take shape on the basis only of the law of the European Union and the European Convention. In addition to the laws of the EU and of the ECHR there is a third structure, that of the domestic laws of each country. The domestic legal systems of the various States influence each other reciprocally and draw ever closer to each other. European

---

[13] Convention for the Protection of Human Rights and Fundamental Freedoms, 4 November 1950, 213 UNTS 221.

law draws inspiration and nourishment from exchanges and interactions between the domestic legal systems of Europe.

Out of these three legal structures—the law of the European Union, the law of the European Convention, and the laws of the different countries of Europe—emerges the path that leads towards a European public law.

2

The Phases of European Integration

The law of nations should be based on a federalism of free states.
—Immanuel Kant, *Perpetual Peace* (1795)

The process of establishing the European project has developed by degrees since its beginnings in the wake of the Second World War; it has not developed without difficulties or crises. But the movement has been stronger than the crises by which it has been beset. European integration has progressed around three axes.

The first follows the development of the European Coal and Steel Community (ECSC) into the European Union (EU), which today is made up of twenty-eight States and accounts for some 508 million inhabitants. The second is that of greater Europe, brought together in the first instance by the European Convention for the Protection of Human Rights and Fundamental Freedoms[1] in the Council of Europe, spanning forty-seven States, among which are all the Member States of the European Union and some 820 million inhabitants. In addition to these two axes comes a third: other more modest European institutions, which nonetheless have contributed more or less permanently to the European cement, especially by associating with the development of European States which are not members of the two great blocs of the European Union and the Council of Europe.

[1] Convention for the Protection of Human Rights and Fundamental Freedoms, 4 November 1950, 213 UNTS 221.

Towards a European Public Law. First Edition. Bernard Stirn. © Bernard Stirn 2017. Published 2017 by Oxford University Press.

1. FROM THE EUROPEAN COAL AND STEEL COMMUNITY TO THE EUROPEAN UNION

Influenced by figures who believed in the European ideal—the 'founding fathers', named by reference to the founding fathers of the United States of America[2]—the constitutive Treaties were adopted in the period 1951–57. Through enlargement and institutional evolutions, the Treaties developed from the first community, the European Coal and Steel Community, into the European Union.

The Founding Fathers

The name 'founding fathers' refers to five men whose concerted efforts were to lay down the foundation stones of the European edifice: the German Chancellor, Konrad Adenauer; the President of the Italian Council, Alcide De Gasperi; the Belgian Prime Minister, Paul-Henri Spaak; and the Frenchmen Jean Monnet and Robert Schuman. Each of them born in the last quarter of the nineteenth century, they drew their European convictions from what was already significant experience. Four were holders of elected office, of whom three were Christian Democrats and one was a Socialist. The last was a businessman and an international financier. Across their differing personal trajectories, all had acquired the same conviction regarding the necessity of a union of the European countries.

Konrad Adenauer was born in 1876 in Cologne, where he became mayor in 1917. A Rhinelander, he belonged to the *Zentrum*, the Catholic centre, and opposed from the beginning the rise of Nazism. Interned several times during the war, after liberation he presided over the new Christian Democratic Union (CDU), becoming in 1949 the first Chancellor of the Federal Republic of Germany, an office he would continue to hold until 1963. His work for the European project

---

[2] John Adams, Benjamin Franklin, Alexander Hamilton, John Jay, Thomas Jefferson, James Madison, and George Washington.

and for Franco–German reconciliation was determined; it culminated in the Élysée Treaty, signed on 22 January 1963,[3] which crowned the strong friendship of Konrad Adenauer with General de Gaulle.

The first political actions of Alcide De Gasperi, born in 1881 in the Trentino, then a dependency of the Austro–Hungarian Empire, had as their aim the reintegration of his native province into Italy. He was a deputy for the Trentino in the Austrian chamber in 1911, and then an Italian deputy in 1921, at which point and following the First World War the Trentino re-joined Italy. President of the Italian People's Party, a Catholic political force, De Gasperi was resolute in his opposition to fascism. He was imprisoned and later banished from political life under Mussolini, and after the war he became Secretary General of the Christian Democrats. From 1945 to 1953 he was the Prime Minister of eight successive governments.

Paul-Henri Spaak, born in 1899 in Brussels and a lawyer by trade, entered Parliament as a Socialist deputy and in 1932 sat briefly in the Belgian government as Minister of Justice and then as Foreign Minister. After becoming Prime Minister in 1938, and becoming Foreign Minister again in 1939, he left for London together with other members of the cabinet following the capitulation of Belgium in 1940. In the aftermath of the war, he once again became Foreign Minister in 1945; he then either led or belonged to every Belgian government until 1957, when he became Secretary General of NATO, having played a leading role in every phase of the development of the European project.

Born in 1886 to a family from Lorraine settled in Luxembourg, Robert Schuman was elected deputy for Moselle in 1919 on a so-called Popular Democrat ticket. A member of the Resistance who was imprisoned by the Nazis, he escaped and assisted in the creation of the Popular Republican Movement, of which he was one of the leading figures when the war was over. Franco–German reconciliation

---

[3] Co-operation Treaty between France and Germany, 22 January 1963, 821 UNTS 323.

was his foremost aim. Having been Prime Minister in 1947–48, he was Foreign Minister when he moved the French government to pass the Schuman Declaration on 9 May 1950, giving expression to the concrete, empirical, and progressive approach which he proposed to follow:

> Europe will not be made all at once, or according to a single plan. It will be built through concrete achievements which first create a *de facto* solidarity. The coming together of the nations of Europe requires the elimination of the age-old opposition of France and Germany. Any action taken must in the first place concern these two countries. With this aim in view, the French Government proposes that action be taken immediately on one limited but decisive point. It proposes that Franco–German production of coal and steel as a whole be placed under a common High Authority, within the framework of an organization open to the participation of the other countries of Europe…. The solidarity in production thus established will make it plain that any war between France and Germany becomes not merely unthinkable, but materially impossible.

In 1985 the Milan European Council decided to make 9 May—the day of the Schuman Declaration—Europe Day.

Jean Monnet is the only founding father of Europe never to have held political office in his country. Born in 1888, he was the head of a family business producing cognac, which led him to travel widely abroad. From this he drew the conviction that international economic exchanges were the wellspring of development and the foundation of peace. Monnet, a businessman and a talented financier, worked successfully for both French and foreign governments. In the USA, where he had the ear of Franklin Roosevelt, he contributed during the Second World War to the establishment of the American armaments industry. After liberation he was the first High Commissioner for the Plan of Modernization and Equipment between 1947 and 1952.

The reconstruction of France was for Monnet indissociable from the construction of Europe. Having been an inspiration to the Schuman Declaration, he was from 1952 to 1955 the first president of the High Authority of the new ECSC.

The Constitutive Treaties

The development of the European Union began with the Treaty of Paris of 18 April 1951,[4] which instituted the first Community: the European Coal and Steel Community. According to its terms, it was concluded to last for fifty years.

Putting into practice the Schuman Declaration, the Treaty of Paris regulated two materials which were at that time symbolic and essential in the economy of the period; in the spirit of the Schuman Declaration, Europe began to constitute itself on the basis of highly concrete realities.

In terms of the choices made, the ECSC would to a large degree prefigure the future European edifice. To begin with, the treaty was concluded between six States: Germany, France, Italy, and the three Benelux countries, Belgium, the Netherlands, and Luxembourg. The United Kingdom, in particular, preferred at this stage not to participate in the movement. Europe took the shape of a Europe of Six, a configuration it would keep until its first enlargement in 1973.

The ECSC was founded on economic principles—a common market, free competition, the fight against abuses of dominant market positions, and merger controls—all of which were relied on to inspire the European project in the long run. Furthermore, the innovative organization of the ECSC outlined the future landscape of the European Community, and later Union, on the basis of the original layout of four institutions: the High Authority, the Special Council of Ministers, the Common Assembly, and the Court of Justice.

[4] Treaty Establishing the European Coal and Steel Community, 18 April 1951, 261 UNTS 140.

The High Authority was the central element of the new Community. Its nine members enjoyed complete independence vis-à-vis the States which appointed them by common agreement. Tasked with setting out and enforcing the general interest of the Community, it had real decision-making power. The future European Commission would be based on the High Authority. In the period 1952–55 Jean Monnet was its first president.

More traditional was the Special Council of Ministers, which gathered the ministers of Member States in areas of Community competence. A Common Assembly was also put in place, with consultative powers only. Finally, a court of the Community was set up, the Court of Justice, composed of seven judges and two Advocates General, inspired largely by the French Conseil d'État. In particular, the Advocates General emulated the *Commissaire du gouvernement* (a sort of unbiased judge rapporteur whose function was to present arguments to the court in the interests of the law, and not in the interest of either of the parties, whether the government or the citizen[5]).

The institutions of the ECSC merged in 1965 with those of the two other Communities created by the Treaty of Rome.[6] In 1992, with the Treaty of Maastricht,[7] the European Community succeeded the three initial communities. The ECSC disappeared completely in 2002, as the Treaty of Paris expired at the end of its fifty years, becoming instead the European Union.

With the decisions of the High Authority binding both Member States and its own court, in addition to creating a dialogue between different institutions, the ECSC represented from the outset a new departure in placing a premium on law, conceived of as one of the foundations of the European edifice. 'Europe was constituted on the basis of a treaty and numerous judgments.... The language of law

---

[5] LN Brown and J Bell, *French Administrative Law* (5th edn, OUP 1998) 49 and 104–6.

[6] Treaty Establishing the European Economic Community, 25 March 1957, 298 UNTS 3.

[7] Treaty on European Union, 7 February 1992, 1757 UNTS 3, [1992] OJ C224/1.

is an integral part of its very being', writes Luuk van Middelaar in *The Passage to Europe*.[8] The High Authority represented, within its domain, a stronger supranational undertaking than that expressed in 1957 by the two Treaties of Rome; but the European construction still bore the mark of the ECSC, the beginning of the project.

An important step was made with the adoption on 25 March 1957 of the two Treaties of Rome,[9] on the basis of the conclusions arrived at in 1955 during the Conference of Messina. This created the two other Communities: the European Economic Community (EEC) and the European Atomic Energy Community (Euratom).

These three communities spanned the same six States: Germany, France, Italy, Belgium, the Netherlands, and Luxembourg.

The object of the European Atomic Energy Community is to organize procurement in the nuclear sector and to develop civil nuclear industry. Military use of nuclear energy remains outside the scope of the organization.

The European Economic Community had a broader horizon. According to the Preamble of its constitutive treaty, it aims to 'lay the foundations of an ever closer union among the peoples of Europe'.[10]

The institutions—the Commission, the Council of Ministers, the Parliamentary Assembly, and the Court of Justice—would at this stage definitively take shape. Based on more of an inter-State approach than the ECSC, decision-making power within the European Economic Community was conferred principally on the Council of Ministers. During the course of the transition period, spanning twelve years, a growing proportion of the decisions of the Council of Ministers was adopted unanimously. In addition to its role as the guarantor of the general interest of the Community, the Commission was given sole

---

[8] I. van Middelaar, *The Passage to Europe: How a Continent Became a Union* (Yale University Press 2013). ('L'Europe s'est constituée à partir d'un traité et de nombreuses décisions ... La langue juridique fait partie intégrante de son être'.)

[9] Treaty Establishing the European Economic Community, 25 March 1957, 298 UNTS 3.

[10] ibid first recital.

power in terms of proposing legislation. The competences of the Court of Justice and the Parliamentary Assembly reach across all three Communities. The power of control over the Commission was given to the Parliamentary Assembly, composed of delegates from the national assemblies: but the possibility of the delegates being elected instead through universal suffrage was not off the cards.

In this period the essential principles—a customs union with a common external tariff; free movement of persons, goods, services, and capital; the guarantee of free competition—were affirmed and a road map for their progressive implementation was set out. Plans for common policies—on commerce, transport, agriculture—were hammered out. At the legal level, secondary legislation would make its appearance in the form of Regulations and Directives.

Having entered into force on 1 January 1958, the two Treaties of Rome were in no way called into question by General de Gaulle on his return to power in France. The customs union had already become effective on 1 January 1958, in advance of the timeline envisaged in the treaty.

A first crisis came about in July 1965, in connection with the recourse to qualified majority voting regarding common agricultural policy. It led to France adopting, for six months, the policy of the empty chair until the adoption on 29 January 1966 of the Luxembourg Compromise, according to which, even beyond the transition period, a State could demand unanimity on an issue if it considered that its essential interests were at stake.

In successive degrees, marked by difficulties which would in turn give way to new prospects, the process set in motion by the six founding countries transformed in half a century the original Communities into a European Union of much grander dimensions and ambitions.

Enlargement

The question of the United Kingdom joining was a live one from the first years of the Community's existence. Sceptical as to the pertinence of the project, the United Kingdom government at first concentrated on the creation of a large area of free trade in Europe; this was manifested in the initiation by the United Kingdom of the European Free Trade Agreement (EFTA) in 1960.[11] When the United Kingdom later expressed its willingness to join the Communities, General de Gaulle registered opposition in 1961 and then again in 1967. Thus it was only after the election in 1969 of Georges Pompidou to the presidency of the French Republic—and the electoral victory of the Conservative government of Edward Heath in 1970—that it became possible for the United Kingdom to join.

Signed in 1972, the first treaty of enlargement concerned the United Kingdom, Ireland, Denmark, and Norway. After a referendum which rejected membership, however, Norway remained outside the European edifice. In France the referendum of 23 April 1972, which was characterized by a high level of abstention (39.31 per cent), nevertheless clearly authorized the ratification of the treaty (67.71 per cent Yes votes). On 1 January 1973 the membership of the Communities went from being six- to nine-strong.

The return of the countries of Mediterranean Europe to democracy paved the way for the accession to the Communities of Greece (1981) and later Spain and Portugal (1986). After the fall of the Berlin Wall (9 November 1989), Austria, Sweden and Finland in 1995 joined the European Community, which had by then succeeded the three communities, whereas Norway, owing to another negative referendum in November 1994, elected once more to remain outside. A new dimension was introduced with the entry of ten new States on 1 May 2004: Poland, Hungary, the Czech Republic, Slovakia, Slovenia, Lithuania, Latvia, Estonia, Cyprus, and Malta. Bulgaria and Romania in turn joined on 1 January 2007. The last country to join was Croatia, which entered on 1 July 2013, making the number of Member States twenty-eight.

---

[11] Convention Establishing the European Free Trade Association, 4 January 1960, 370 UNTS 5.

Although no new entrants are envisaged in the short term, the frontiers of the Union are not definitively fixed. Negotiations have been ongoing with Turkey since 2005. Albania, Macedonia, Montenegro, and Serbia are candidates. Iceland had even applied before it 'froze' its application in 2014, and then withdrew it in March 2015. Bosnia Herzegovina and Kosovo are recognized as potential candidates. There is an open question as to certain Eastern European countries, primarily Ukraine, as well as Georgia and Moldova.

The Treaty of Lisbon[12] formalized the rules of accession, by providing in Article 49 of the Treaty for the Functioning of the European Union (TFEU) both the substantive requirements and procedures for accession. Any 'European State' may apply to become a member: this geographical criterion, which in 1987 led to Morocco's candidature being dismissed, is perhaps the most difficult to apply to countries which, like Turkey, are only partly situated on the European continent.

Accession is conditional on compliance with the criteria defined by the June 1993 European Council in Copenhagen:[13] membership requires respect for and promotion of the values of the European Union, a political regime that has achieved stability of institutions guaranteeing democracy, the existence of a functioning market economy, and acceptance of the *acquis communautaire*. In procedural terms the application is addressed to the Council, which must decide unanimously, on the advice of the Commission, to grant the application or not. The European Parliament and the national parliaments are informed of the decision. The accession is then concluded decisively by a treaty needing ratification by all Member States.

Article 50 of the Treaty on the Functioning of the European Union gives every State Member the right to withdraw from the Union. The

---

[12] Amending the Treaty on European Union and the Treaty Establishing the European Community, 13 December 2007, [2007] OJ C306/1.
[13] Bulletin of the European Communities, No 6/1993.

process of withdrawal provides that the Union, through the Council, acting by a qualified majority, and after obtaining the consent of the European Parliament, shall negotiate and conclude an agreement with the withdrawing State setting out the arrangements for the withdrawal. The affirmation in the treaty of the right to withdraw underscores that the Union cannot be likened to a federal state, of which the members may not in principle secede. If this affirmation is mostly theoretical, it has nonetheless contributed to the debates on the possibility of the withdrawal from the EU of Greece—Grexit—in the context of the debt crisis, and indeed of the United Kingdom—Brexit—after the 23 June 2016 referendum promised by David Cameron. A Member State may not, however, be excluded from the Union. At most some rights, including voting rights, could be suspended pursuant to Article 7 TFEU, if a serious and persistent violation of the fundamental values of the Union were found to have occurred, following a complex procedure initiated by the Council by a four-fifths majority.

Institutional Development

As it has enlarged, the institutional structure of the European project has undergone constant development.

The first modifications of the Treaties were of an ad hoc nature. In 1965 the executive branches of the three Communities were conjoined, becoming one Council of Ministers and one Commission. The Treaty of Luxembourg in 1970 allocated the European Economic Community funds of its own.

An evolution of a different kind followed in the wake of the constitution of the European Council, decided in 1974, without treaty change having been necessary at that time, at the behest of President Valéry Giscard d'Estaing and Chancellor Helmut Schmidt. The European Council consists of a regular meeting, at least twice per year, of heads of state or governments of the Member States, assisted by ministers of foreign affairs, which is also attended by the president and a member

of the Commission. According to the terms of the Declaration instituting the European Council, the Council 'provides a general political impetus to the construction of Europe'.[14] The European Council
lays out the broad lines, which the Council of Ministers and the
Commission then implement. Although it is the decisive provider
of political impetus for the construction of Europe, the European
Council was inscribed into the treaties only in the Single European
Act and the Treaty of Maastricht.

A new institution, the European Court of Auditors, was created in
1975, when the European Parliament gained budgetary powers. In
1976 it was decided that the European Parliament was to be elected
directly by universal suffrage, the voting procedures being set out by
each State. The first election took place in June 1979. Simone Veil,
a former government minister under President Giscard d'Estaing,
became the new Parliament's first president.

With this deepening of the construction of Europe, a renovation of
the whole of the institutional system became necessary. Having been
made President of the European Commission in 1985, Jacques Delors
took it upon himself to finalize the projects already underway in that
connection; this led to the Single European Act and then the Treaty
of Maastricht.

Adopted in February 1986, the Single European Act,[15] so named
because it was meant to govern the entirety of Community matters,
provided for the realization—ahead of 1 January 1993—of the com-
pletion of the internal market, without internal frontiers.[16] In order
to put in place this great internal market, numerous harmoniza-
tion measures were taken with a view to removing barriers—physical, technical, or fiscal—which still impaired the total freedom of
movement of persons, products, capital, and services. New common

[14] Solemn Declaration on European Union, European Council, 19 June 1983,
Bulletin of the European Communities, No 6/1983 at [2.1.2].
[15] Bulletin of the European Communities, No 6/1987 at [2.4.5].
[16] See Art 13 of the Single European Act.

policies were decided, in the fields of economic and social cohesion, the environment, and research.

At the institutional level, the Single Act changed the voting procedure to qualified majority, expanded—especially by way of the co-operation procedure—the powers of the European Parliament (which the Single Act officially gave that title, instead of the Common Assembly), and reinforced the European Council institutionally. Finally, it opened up an avenue of co-operation in the context of foreign policy. The Single Act would prefigure the Treaty of Maastricht, which was signed on 7 February 1992 and which entered into force after ratification by all twelve Member States on 1 November 1993, a process which at times proved difficult.[17]

Opening up the European project to new prospects, the Treaty of Maastricht transformed the European Economic Community into the European Community. With the ECSC and Euratom, this Community would form the central community pillar, to which two new pillars were added, both intergovernmental: one concerning Common Foreign and Security Policy, and the other concerning Justice and Home Affairs. Although at this stage it lacked legal personality, the European Union was created. The contours of a European citizenry began to emerge, in due course leading the Court of Justice to affirm that 'citizenship of the Union is intended to be the fundamental status of nationals of the Member States'.[18] It led to a right to petition the European Parliament and gave every citizen of the Union the right to vote in their country of residence in municipal elections and elections to the European Parliament. The powers of the European Parliament were reinforced, especially with the introduction of the co-decision procedure. New policies were devised, in the fields of education, culture, health, consumer protection, while the principle of subsidiarity was strengthened.

---

[17] Treaty on European Union, 7 February 1992, 1757 UNTS 3, [1992] OJ C224/1.
[18] Case C–184/99 *Rudy Grzelczyk v Centre public d'aide sociale d'Ottignies-Louvain-la-Neuve* ECLI:EU:C:2001:458 at [31].

The Treaty of Maastricht set the construction of Europe on a course towards an economic and monetary Union. This led to co-ordination of economic policies and created the possibility—with a network constituted of independent national central banks and of a future European central bank—of the adoption of a single currency. Effectively in place from 1 January 1999, the euro was on 1 January 2002 substituted for the domestic currencies of the Eurozone countries.

By setting the European project on a path towards what was plainly closer integration, the Maastricht Treaty caused heated political disagreement, often couched in constitutional terms.

In its decision of 9 April 1992, the French Conseil constitutionnel, in a case referred to it by the President of the French Republic, decided that the treaty had a bearing on three essential conditions of the exercise of national sovereignty: the conferral on Union citizens of the right to vote and stand as a candidate in local elections in the Member State in which he or she resided, the prospect of the adoption of a single currency, and the abandonment of the rule of unanimity—with the introduction of qualified majority voting—for the determination of the rules regulating the issuance of visas to third country nationals, allowing them to enter the territory of the European Union.[19] A constitutional revision was therefore a necessary prerequisite for ratification of the treaty. Adopted on 25 June 1992, this revision brought Europe into the French Constitution, by adding to the text of the Constitution what would, through the constitutional statute of 4 February 2008, eventually become Chapter XV *On the European Union*. With the constitutional hurdles passed, the statute authorizing the ratification of the Treaty of Maastricht was put to a referendum on 20 September 1992. Mobilizing the electorate, with a turnout of 70 per cent, the referendum produced a close result, Yes winning with 51.05 per cent.

---

[19] *Re Treaty on European Union, 1992* (Maastricht I) (1992) 93 ILR 337.

Several other European countries—especially Belgium, Denmark, Germany, Ireland, Italy, Portugal, and Spain—experienced similar political and constitutional debates. On 1 July 1992 the Spanish Constitutional Tribunal decided that the right to vote in municipal elections could not be given to European citizens without a constitutional amendment, which was in due course adopted on 30 July 1993. The German Federal Constitutional Court, deciding on the constitutionality of the statute ratifying the Maastricht Treaty, also held that a modification of the domestic constitution was necessary, in its decision of 12 October 1993.[20] In total, the ratification of the Treaty of Maastricht necessitated constitutional revision in five of the twelve Member States: France, Ireland, Portugal, and Spain in 1992; Germany in 1993. Other than in France, referenda were organized in Ireland, on 18 June 1992 (68.70 per cent Yes), and, twice, in Denmark, where, after a negative referendum on 2 June 1992, the Yes vote finally carried the day, with 58.80 per cent of the votes, on 18 May 1993. These constitutional revisions and referenda serve to underscore the particular impact of the Treaty of Maastricht.

What had been begun in the Treaty of Maastricht would continue in the Treaty of Amsterdam of 2 October 1997.[21] This treaty amended the co-decision procedure, increasing the power of the European Parliament. It added to the objectives of the EU the establishment of the area of 'Freedom, Security, and Justice', which became part of the third pillar of the European Union. Finally, it allowed some States to engage in certain kinds of expanded co-operation, in which not all States were prepared to engage. All of the institutional problems connected to enlargement were, however, far from resolved. Without making systemic changes, the Treaty of Nice,[22] signed in February 2001, made certain improvements.

---

[20] *Maastricht Treaty 1992 Constitutionality Case* (1993) 98 ILR 196.

[21] Amending the TEU, the Treaties Establishing the European Communities and Certain Related Acts, 2 October 1997, [1997] OJ C340/1.

[22] Amending the TEU, the Treaties Establishing the European Communities and Certain Related Acts, 26 February 2001, [2001] OJ C80/1.

It was also at Nice that, in December 2000, the European Council adopted the Charter of Fundamental Rights of the European Union.[23]

The elaboration of this reference document—which gave the European Union a whole new dimension in the field of safeguarding rights and liberties—was decided by the European Councils of Cologne (June 1999) and Tampere (October 1999). An initial procedure had been conceived for the development of the document, entrusted to a 'body', later to rename itself a 'Convention', consisting of national government representatives, the President of the Commission, and members of national parliaments and the European Parliament. Presided over by a former president of the German Federal Constitutional Court, Roman Herzog, the Convention succeeded (owing in no small measure to the conciliatory efforts of one of its vice presidents, the Frenchman Guy Braibant, a senior judge in the Conseil d'État, and also those of the UK member, Lord Goldsmith QC) in finalizing a text which gave expression to the shared values of the Union. In six chapters—dignity, freedoms, equality, solidarity, citizens' rights, and justice—the Charter adopts the principles set out by the European Convention on Human Rights, although it has a broader ambit than the European Convention. On the one hand, it deals with recent concerns such as the environment and bioethics; on the other hand, it deals not only with political and civil rights but also economic and social ones.

After its proclamation by the European Council, the Charter was the object of an inter-institutional agreement between the Council, the Parliament, and the Commission. It became positive law on its incorporation—together with certain modifications adopted at Strasbourg in December 2007—into the Treaty of Lisbon.

---

[23] Charter of Fundamental Rights of the European Union, 7 December 2000, [2000] OJ C364/1.

The Charter furnished the European Union with something like a constitutional preamble. Thus it logically led to the idea of a constitutional treaty, which would transform all of the EU institutions and give them the necessary foundation. The use of Conventions, which had been so effective in connection with the Charter, was retained in December 2001 by the European Council at Laeken. Presided over by former French President Valéry Giscard d'Estaing, the new Convention had in July 2003, after eighteen months of work, finished drafting the Treaty establishing a Constitution for Europe.[24] But France and the Netherlands rejected the treaty in their referenda during the spring of 2005, leading to the project being abandoned.

A recasting of all of the treaties then began. It resulted in the Treaty of Lisbon, signed on 13 December 2007,[25] entering into force on 1 December 2009 having been ratified by all the Member States.

The Treaty of Lisbon is composed of two instruments, the Treaty on European Union (TEU), which sets out certain constitutional principles for the EU, and the Treaty on the Functioning of the European Union (TFEU), which determines the competences of the institutions and lays down the ways in which they function. The three pillars—the Communities, Common Foreign and Security Policy, and Justice and Home Affairs—became one. The Charter of Fundamental Rights was given the same status as the treaty. The European Union succeeded the legal personality of the European Communities. The values and fundamental principles on which the Union was founded were affirmed; at the same time, however, what emerged was a profoundly reformed institutional organization.

---

[24] Treaty Establishing a Constitution for Europe, 29 October 2004, [2004] OJ C310/1 (never entered into force).

[25] Treaty of Lisbon Amending the Treaty of European Union and the Treaty Establishing the European Community, 13 December 2007, [2007] OJ C306/1. Also: Consolidated Versions of the Treaty on European Union and the Treaty on the Functioning of the European Union, [2012] OJ C326.

2. THE COUNCIL OF EUROPE AND
THE EUROPEAN CONVENTION FOR
THE PROTECTION OF HUMAN RIGHTS
AND FUNDAMENTAL FREEDOMS

In 1948 the Hague Congress was convened with a view to reflect on the future of Europe in the wake of the war. Eminent political figures of all stripes participated: Winston Churchill, Léon Blum, Paul Reynaud, Robert Schuman, Jean Monnet, Alcide De Gasperi, and Paul-Henri Spaak. The discussions resulted, on 5 May 1949, in the Treaty of London,[26] which created the first European organization: the Council of Europe. This organization initially spanned ten States—Belgium, Denmark, France, Ireland, Italy, Luxembourg, Norway, the Netherlands, Sweden, and the United Kingdom. The institutional system of the Council of Europe was original; its work would be based on the rule of law and the respect for fundamental rights, especially on the European Convention for the Protection of Human Rights and Fundamental Freedoms, signed in the heart of Europe, at Rome, on 4 November 1950. The Council of Europe has since gone through substantial enlargement, with a view to covering all of 'greater Europe'. It now spans forty-seven States, accounting for 800 million inhabitants.

The Institutions of the Council of Europe

With its seat in Strasbourg, the Council of Europe consists of a Parliamentary Assembly, a Committee of Ministers, and a Secretary General. The first assembly to have been set up at the European level, the Parliamentary Assembly of the Council of Europe is composed of 318 members, appointed by national parliaments. The number of representatives varies from two to eighteen per country, according

---

[26] Statute of the Council of Europe ('Treaty of London'), 5 May 1949, 87 UNTS 103, ETS 1.

to demographics. Sitting for four annual sessions each of which lasts for a week, the Parliamentary Assembly debates important topical issues and makes recommendations to the Committee of Ministers. Its deliberations are prepared by commissions. The Assembly elects the Secretary General as well as the judges of the European Court of Human Rights.

The Committee of Ministers, the foremost decision-making body, gathers the ministers of foreign affairs of the Member States at least twice each year. Its rotating presidency is held for six months by the minister of each State, according to an alphabetic rotation. The Committee decides the budget of the Council of Europe. It supervises the States' compliance with the commitments they have undertaken within the framework of the organization, and the enforcement of judgments handed down by the European Court of Human Rights. It decides by unanimous agreement. Between its sessions, ambassadors representing the States in the Council of Europe meet weekly.

Elected by the Parliamentary Assembly for a renewable mandate of five years, the Secretary General is responsible for the strategic management of the institution.

Rule of Law and Respect for Fundamental Rights

With the vocation of ensuring the respect for the rule of law in Europe, the Council of Europe's first achievement was the European Convention for the Protection of Human Rights and Fundamental Freedoms, and the European Court of Human Rights is the pivot of its activity.

It also carries on other activities, especially in connection with different international treaty regimes, the Commissioner for Human Rights and various other organs.

The European Convention for the Protection of Human Rights and Fundamental Freedoms, European Convention on Human Rights (ECHR) for short, was adopted in 1950 against the backdrop of the victory over Nazism. Its object was to establish a mechanism of collective guarantees of fundamental rights. The Convention safeguards certain absolute rights, such as the right to life (Article 2), the prohibition of torture and inhuman or degrading treatment (Article 3), and the prohibition of slavery and forced labour (Article 4). The other rights set out by the Convention can be restricted only when the restriction, provided for by law, is necessary in a democratic society.

This is particularly the case with the right to liberty and security (Article 5); the right to a fair trial (Article 6); the right to respect for private and family life (Article 8); freedom of thought, conscience, and religion (Article 9); freedom of expression (Article 10); freedom of assembly and association (Article 11); and the right to an effective remedy (Article 13).

Sixteen additional protocols complement the Convention. Especially important are Protocol 1,[27] which concerns the protection of property; Protocols 6[28] and 13,[29] relating to the abolition of the death penalty; and Protocols 11[30] and 14,[31] which have profoundly changed the procedure of intervention before the European Court of Human Rights. Protocol 15,[32] which codifies the principle of subsidiarity and the so-called national margin of appreciation, and Protocol 16,[33] which allows highest courts and tribunals to request the Strasbourg Court to give advisory opinions on questions of principle relating to the interpretation or application of the Convention, both adopted in 2013, are in the process of being ratified.

Although the text of the Convention owed much to René Cassin— an intimate of General de Gaulle's in London from June 1940, Vice President of the Conseil d'État in the period 1944–60, and Nobel Peace Prize laureate in 1968—France was slow to ratify the

---

[27] ETS 9—Human Rights (Protocol No 1), 20 March 1952.
[28] ETS 114—Human Rights (Protocol No 6), 28 April 1983.
[29] ETS 187—Human Rights (Protocol No 13), 3 May 2002.
[30] ETS 155—Human Rights (Protocol No 11), 11 May 1994.
[31] ETS 194—Human Rights (Protocol No 14), 13 May 2004.
[32] ETS 213—Human Rights (Protocol No 15), 24 June 2013.
[33] ETS 214—Human Rights (Protocol No 16), 2 November 2013.

Convention. A concatenation of reasons explains the French reserve in this regard. On the one hand, it was feared that France's attitude in the conflicts of decolonization, in Indochina and later in Algeria, might be challenged. On the other hand, there were misgivings of principle about an international mechanism for the protection of human rights; the country of the Declaration of the Rights of Man and of the Citizen 1789 thought it had no use. In vain, René Cassin— who was a judge and then, in 1965, president of the Court while France had still not ratified the Convention—observed that adhering to the Convention would be 'the price to pay if we want to lead by example'.

Authorized by statute on 31 December 1973, ratification by France was pronounced by decree on 3 May 1974, signed by President Alain Poher, during his caretaker presidency after the death of President Pompidou. But still France did not accept the right of individual petition of French citizens to the Court, which was not obligatory until 2 October 1981.

One of the new initiatives and strengths of the European Convention on Human Rights was the creation of a court of law, the European Court of Human Rights, composed of one judge from each State. Having come into operation in 1959, the European Court handed down its first judgment on 14 November 1960.[34]

The judges of the Court are elected for non-renewable mandates of nine years by the Council of Europe's Parliamentary Assembly, from a list of three candidates put forward by the States. They cannot sit beyond the age of seventy years. Protocol 15 replaces that age-limit by a rule according to which a judge must be below sixty-five when he or she is elected. The judges elect their president, for a non-renewable mandate of three years.

After the exhaustion of domestic remedies, the Court may, within six months from the date on which the final domestic decision was

---

[34] *Lawless v Ireland (No 1)* (1961) 31 ILR 290, (1979–80) 1 EHRR 1.

taken,[35] deal with any breach of the Convention. Being subsidiary in relation to the procedures taking place before domestic courts, the Convention is in this way directly accessible for individuals.

Within the framework of inter-State cases, a State may also refer to the Court any alleged breach of the Convention which it considers attributable to another State Member. This type of recourse to the Court by States has remained exceptional. Ireland in the 1970s brought a case against the United Kingdom on the subject of security measures in Northern Ireland.[36] Cyprus and Turkey have confronted one another over the situation in Northern Cyprus.[37] During the conflict in 2008 between Georgia and Russia, Georgia referred to the Court an inter-State case against Russia.[38] The tensions between Russia and Ukraine led to three cases between them being filed in 2014.[39]

Finally, at the instigation of the Council of Europe's Committee of Ministers, the Court can give advisory opinions on legal questions concerning the interpretation of the Convention and its protocols. This procedure has been used only three times.[40]

With the entry into force of Protocol 11 in 1998, the Court, which until then sat for no more than a few sessions per year, took on a permanent character; the right to individual petition, until then optional, became obligatory. At this point the European Commission of Human Rights, which until then would filter the applications received, disappeared; the whole system became court-based. Having entered into force on 1 June 2010, Protocol 14 changed and lightened

---

[35] Protocol 15 reduces this period to four months.

[36] *Ireland v United Kingdom* (1978) 58 ILR 188, (1979–80) 2 EHRR 25.

[37] *Cyprus v Turkey* (2001) 120 ILR 10, (2002) 35 EHRR 30; *Cyprus v Turkey* (2014) 159 ILR 1, (2014) 59 EHRR 16.

[38] *Georgia v Russia (Admissibility)* (2011) 161 ILR 487, (2011) 52 EHRR SE14.

[39] *Ukraine v Russia I–IV* (App Nos 20958/14, 43800/14, 49537/14, and 42410/15).

[40] Decision on the competence of the Court to give an Advisory Opinion ECHR 2004–VI p 271; Advisory Opinion on certain legal questions concerning the lists of candidates submitted with a view to the election of judges to the European Court of Human Rights (No 1) (unreported) 12 February 2008; Advisory Opinion on certain legal questions concerning the lists of candidates submitted with a view to the election of judges to the European Court of Human Rights (No 2) (unreported) 22 January 2010.

the procedure with a view to allowing the Court better to deal with the growing number of cases filed with it.

Through the European Court of Human Rights, the Convention took on a 'special character as a treaty for the collective enforcement of human rights and fundamental freedoms'.[41] This characterization is all the more important since the Court applies the principles of the Convention firmly and constructively, interpreting its provisions in an open, dynamic, flexible, and evolutionary manner.[42] For the members of the European Union, the rights set out by the Convention apply in conjunction with those flowing from the law of the Union.

Other than the European Convention on Human Rights, the Council of Europe has initiated through its diplomatic activities a number of important treaties, the common denominator of which is both the promotion of the enjoyment of fundamental rights, and to fight at the European level against the setbacks the European project has experienced.

Adopted by the Committee of Ministers and the Parliamentary Assembly, these treaties do not by themselves bind the state; they become binding only on States which ratify them. Many of them have been called Charters, which corresponds to their purpose of setting out essential guarantees, while also leaving the State a broad margin of appreciation in terms of their implementation.

One of the most important is the European Social Charter,[43] adopted in 1961 and revised in 1996. It establishes a full range of social rights; provides that each State Party reports, every year, on the implementation of the rights; and institutes, with a view to supervising the fulfilment by the States of its principles, the European Committee of Social Rights, composed of fifteen members who are elected by the

---

[41] *Ireland v United Kingdom* (1978) 58 ILR 188, (1979–80) 2 EHRR 25 at [239]; *Soering v United Kingdom* (1989) 98 ILR 270, (1989) 11 EHRR 439 at [87].

[42] See F Moderne, *La Convention européenne des droits de l'homme* (Armand Colin 2005); E Bjorge, *The Evolutionary Interpretation of Treaties* (OUP 2014) 10–14.

[43] European Social Charter, 18 October 1961, ETS No 35; 3 May 1996, ETS No 163.

Committee of Ministers for a mandate of six years, renewable once. The ratification by France, authorized by statute 10 March 1999, was done by decree on 4 February 2000.

By a decree of 3 May 2007, France also ratified the European Charter of Local Self-Government,[44] which was adopted in 1985. This charter led to the establishment of the Congress of Local and Regional Authorities, a consultative assembly which gathers 636 local councillors, representing around 200,000 local and regional authorities from the forty-seven State Members. The Congress evaluates the state of local democracy and adopts resolutions with a view to improving it.

France has signed,[45] but not ratified, the European Charter for Regional or Minority Languages.[46] By its decision of 15 June 1999,[47] the Conseil constitutionnel effectively determined that the charter ran contrary to the constitutional principles of the indivisibility of the French Republic, equality before the law, and the unity of the French people. It also determined that by authorizing the use of a regional language not only in private life but also in dealings with public administration, the charter also amounted to a breach of Article 2 of the Constitution, according to which '[t]he language of the Republic shall be French'. A constitutional revision would, in those circumstances, be necessary if the charter were to be ratified by France. Although the question has been raised from time to time, no procedure has been carried out to this end.

Amongst the other treaties adopted within the framework of the Council of Europe, the following should be mentioned: the European Convention on Extradition (1957);[48] European Convention on the Suppression of Terrorism (1977);[49] Convention for the Protection

---

[44] European Charter of Local Self-Government, 15 October 1985, ETS No 122.

[45] 7 May 1999.

[46] European Charter for Regional or Minority Languages, 5 November 1992, ETS No 148.

[47] Decision No 99–412 of 15 June 1999.

[48] European Convention on Extradition, 13 December 1957, ETS No 024.

[49] European Convention on the Suppression of Terrorism, 27 January 1977, ETS No 090.

of Individuals with regard to Automatic Processing of Personal Data (1981);[50] European Convention for the Prevention of Torture and Inhuman or Degrading Treatment or Punishment (1987);[51] Convention on Human Rights and Biomedicine (1997);[52] Convention on Cybercrime (2001);[53] Convention on Action against Trafficking in Human Beings (2005);[54] Convention on Laundering, Search, Seizure and Confiscation of the Proceeds of Crime and the Financing of Terrorism (2005);[55] Convention on the Protection of Children against Sexual Exploitation and Sexual Abuse (2007);[56] Convention on Preventing and Combating Violence against Women and Domestic Violence (2011);[57] Convention on the Counterfeiting of Medical Products and Similar Crimes Involving Threats to Public Health (2011);[58] and Convention on the Manipulation of Sports Competitions.[59]

Set up in 1999, the Commissioner for Human Rights is elected by the Parliamentary Assembly for a non-renewable mandate of six years. By means of recommendations to the States Members and reports to the Committee of Ministers and the Parliamentary Assembly, the Commissioner is tasked with raising awareness of and promoting respect for human rights. Three commissioners have

---

[50] Convention for the Protection of Individuals with regard to Automatic Processing of Personal Data, 28 January 1981, ETS No 108.

[51] European Convention for the Prevention of Torture and Inhuman or Degrading Treatment or Punishment, 26 November 1987, ETS No 126.

[52] Convention on Human Rights and Biomedicine, 4 April 1997, ETS No 164.

[53] Convention on Cybercrime, 23 November 2001, ETS No 185.

[54] Convention on Action against Trafficking in Human Beings, 16 May 2005, ETS No 197.

[55] Convention on Laundering, Search, Seizure and Confiscation of the Proceeds of Crime and the Financing of Terrorism, 16 May 2005, ETS No 198.

[56] Convention on the Protection of Children against Sexual Exploitation and Sexual Abuse, 25 October 2007, ETS No 201.

[57] Convention on Preventing and Combating Violence against Women and Domestic Violence, 11 May 2011, ETS No 210.

[58] Convention on the Counterfeiting of Medical Products and Similar Crimes Involving Threats to Public Health, 28 October 2011, ETS No 211.

[59] Convention on the Manipulation of Sports Competitions, 18 September 2014, ETS No 215.

exercised these functions: first, the Spaniard Álvaro Gil-Robles, then the Swede Thomas Hammarberg and, since 2012, the Latvian Nils Muižnieks.

Furthermore, the Council of Europe undertakes various activities aimed at consolidating democracy. It has a Development Bank,[60] the seat of which is Paris. The Council of Europe has set up the European Commission for Democracy through Law, better known as the Venice Commission, an advisory body which provides legal advice to States in democratic transition, and especially in connection with the drafting of constitutions and organization of free elections. Finally, the Council of Europe has observer status within the United Nations.

Greater Europe

Originally uniting ten States, the Council of Europe has progressively enlarged over time. In August 1949 Greece and Turkey joined; Germany joined in 1950. Gradually, all of the countries of Europe became members. It is worth mentioning that Austria joined in 1956, Switzerland in 1963, Portugal in 1976, and Spain in 1977.

From 1990 onwards, the countries of Eastern Europe entered, including Russia in 1996. Given its lack of democratic institutions, Belarus remains a non-member. The last entrants were Monaco in 2004 and Montenegro in 2007.

With its forty-seven members, the Council of Europe is the organization of Greater Europe. In addition, it also plays a role in international diplomacy: the USA, Canada, Japan, Mexico, and the Holy See all have observer status within the Council of Europe, while the parliaments of Canada, Israel, and Mexico are observers within its Parliamentary Assembly.

---

[60] The Council of Europe Development Bank (CEB).

3. THE OTHER EUROPEAN INSTITUTIONS

Other than the two central institutions of the European Union and the Council of Europe, other organizations also contribute to the construction of Europe. They can be divided into three categories: first, those which are related to security and the military; secondly, those concerned with commerce and economic development; and thirdly, the Schengen Area and Eurozone, both of which are sub-organizations directly connected with the European Union.

Military Co-operation, Defence, and Security: from the Failure of the European Defence Community to the Organization for Security and Co-operation in Europe

In 1952 the six Member States of the ECSC signed, in Paris, an agreement creating the European Defence Community (EDC). Applying to the military field the model adopted in connection with coal and steel, this ambitious project sought, in the context of the Cold War, on the one hand to allow German rearmament, whilst on the other integrating Germany into the framework of a European army. But the project took for granted a political construction, for which there was no widely held desire. In France debates as to the ratification of the treaty became, in a context of great governmental instability, extremely intense. 'Between January 1953 and August 1954 the greatest ideological-political feud unfolded that France had seen probably since the Dreyfus affair', wrote Raymond Aron.[61] On 30 August 1954, under the government of Pierre Mendès France, the National Assembly refused to authorize ratification.

The failure of the European Defence Community stands as one of the strongly resented vicissitudes of the march towards the European

---

[61] R Aron, *Esquisse historique d'une grande querelle idéologique* (Armand Colin 1956) ('Entre janvier 1953 et août 1954, se déchaîna la plus grande querelle idéologico-politique que la France ait connue probablement depuis l'affaire Dreyfus').

construction; its consequences within the field of defence are still not entirely gone.

In order, nonetheless, to open up a path towards the rearmament of Germany, the Western Union Defence Organization, created by the Treaty of Brussels of 17 March 1948[62] and which united France, the United Kingdom, Belgium, the Netherlands, and Luxembourg, was expanded by the Paris Accords of 23 October 1954 to include Germany and Italy, and took the name the Western European Union (WEU). Germany thus recovered its full sovereignty. The Western European Union spanned the Europe of Six and the United Kingdom. Its institutions were the Council of Foreign Ministers, which made decisions by unanimity, and a Parliamentary Assembly made up of the representatives of the seven Member States in the Parliamentary Assembly of the Council of Europe. As an organization for integration within the field of defence, and one closely connected with NATO, the WEU over time lost its relevance to the European Union, which took over its activities after it was dissolved in June 2011.

Beyond the European framework, the North Atlantic Treaty of 4 April 1949[63] covered at the outset—within NATO, the organization it created—Canada, the USA, and ten European States: Belgium, Denmark, France, Iceland, Italy, Luxembourg, Norway, the Netherlands, Portugal, and the United Kingdom. The organization was conceived in order to secure the defence of the free world in the context of the Cold War. Against this, the Warsaw Pact, including the USSR, was set up as a counterpart to NATO. Over time NATO enlarged: Greece and Turkey joined in 1952, Germany in 1955, Spain in 1982. The nature of the organization changed after the fall of Communist regimes, and in 1999 Hungary, Poland, and the Czech Republic joined. Seven new countries joined them in 2004: Estonia, Latvia, Lithuania, Bulgaria, Romania, Slovakia, and Slovenia, and

---

[62] Treaty for Collaboration in Economic, Social and Cultural Matters and for Collective Self-Defence, 17 March 1948, 19 UNTS 51.

[63] North Atlantic Treaty, 4 April 1949, 34 UNTS 243.

then Albania and Croatia in 2009. NATO thus now counts twenty-eight Member States. Bosnia, Georgia, Montenegro, and Macedonia have stated their aspirations for membership. Ukraine also contemplates doing so, which has raised tensions with Russia. France, while remaining a member of the organization, left the integrated military structure in 1966, and rejoined it in 2009. Now a force for equilibrium and peace, acting closely and in harmony with the UN, NATO has intervened both inside Europe, as in Kosovo in 1999, as well as outside of Europe, such as in Afghanistan and in Libya. It is closely connected with the European Union, with which it concluded an agreement on strategic partnership in 2008.[64]

From the developing relationship between East and West in Europe, the Conference on Security and Co-operation in Europe was born in 1973, within the framework of the 'Helsinki process'. This became in 1994 the Organization for Security and Co-operation in Europe (OSCE). Its initial aim was to facilitate multilateral dialogue between the two parts of Europe and to contribute to the respect of the principles of free movement of persons and ideas in Europe, which had been affirmed by the final act of the Helsinki conference.[65] The organization, the seat of which is in Vienna, has gone from strength to strength, responding to changes in the countries of Central and Eastern Europe, the Caucasus, and Central Asia. Spanning fifty-seven States in Europe, Asia, and North America, the OSCE is the foremost of the regional security organizations. It offers to its members a forum for discussion, contributes to the prevention of conflict, and implements procedures for crisis management. In 2014 it attempted to contribute to allaying the Ukraine crisis by sending observers. It set up a Court of Conciliation and Arbitration, first presided over by the French jurist Robert Badinter, and then by the German jurist Christian Tomuschat since 2013.

---

[64] Bucharest Summit Declaration: see NATO Press Release (2008) 49.

[65] Final Act of the Conference on Security and Co-operation in Europe (1975) 14 ILM 1292.

Commerce and Economic Development:
OECD, EFTA, EEA

In order to implement the Marshall Plan, launched in 1947 by the USA to rebuild Europe, the Organization for European Economic Co-operation (OEEC) was set up on 16 April 1948, becoming in 1961 the Organization for Economic Co-operation and Development (OECD). Through deliberations and recommendations, its mission is to assist the Member States—the number of which has increased from eighteen to thirty-four—in achieving sustainable economic growth. Its intellectual influence is particularly strong on subjects such as debt management, protection of the environment, the fight against tax havens, and development aid. Its seat is in Paris.

The successive enlargement of the European Free Trade Association (EFTA), created in 1960, has led most of its Members States to join the European Union. EFTA continues nonetheless to govern four countries which are not EU members: Iceland, Liechtenstein, Norway, and Switzerland. The first three of those States in 1992 joined the European Economic Area (EEA), to which Switzerland refused to accede, however, by reason of a negative referendum on 6 December 1992. Through the EEA, the free movement of persons, services, goods, and capital is guaranteed between the EU, Iceland, Liechtenstein, and Norway. Sectorial bilateral agreements have been concluded between the EU and Switzerland.

Closely Tied with the European Union:
the Schengen Area and the Eurozone

The Schengen Area

On 14 June 1985, at Schengen in Luxembourg, five States—Germany, Belgium, France, Luxembourg, and the Netherlands—signed agreements aiming to remove border control and to organize police and judicial co-operation in the field of immigration.[66] The Convention

---

[66] Agreement between the States of the Benelux Economic Union, Germany and France on the Gradual Abolition of Checks at their Common Frontiers, OJ L239/13.

Applying the Schengen Agreement,[67] of 19 June 1990, fleshes out the provisions of the Schengen Agreement. Schengen visas of short duration, up to a maximum of three months, were instituted allowing for free movement within all of the Schengen Area. The Schengen Information System (SIS), a joint information system, was also created. Border checks at common frontiers may be temporarily re-established in case of migration pressures which become impossible to control or serious risks to internal security. Decisions concerning asylum are taken in respect of the whole area the moment the individual concerned enters the Schengen Area.

In France the application of the Schengen agreements necessitated a constitutional amendment. Having found, in its decision of 25 July 1991,[68] that the Convention Applying the Schengen Agreement did not call into question fundamental principles of national sovereignty, the Conseil constitutionnel, in its decision of 13 August 1993,[69] in effect censured the legislative instruments implementing the treaty provisions concerning the right to asylum.

The Preamble of the French Constitution, in the same vein as the Montagnard Constitution of 1793, provides that: 'Any man persecuted in virtue of his actions in favour of liberty may claim the right of asylum upon the territories of the Republic.' The exercise of the right to asylum together with other countries as a result necessitated a constitutional revision, which was done on 25 November 1993. Without changing the Preamble, the revision introduced into the Constitution Article 53-1, according to which:

> The Republic may enter into agreements with European States which are bound by undertakings identical with its own in matters of asylum and the protection of human rights and fundamental freedoms, for the purpose of determining their respective jurisdiction as regards requests for asylum submitted to them.

---

[67] Convention Applying the Schengen Agreement, 19 June 1990, [1999] OJ L239/19.
[68] Decision No 91–294 of 25 July 1991.
[69] Decision No 93–325 of 13 August 1993.

Against this background, applications for asylum may, within a European framework, be dealt with by way of joint processing. The second paragraph of Article 53 does however reserve national competence to grant asylum, whatever may have been the position of a partner state, 'to any foreigner who is persecuted for his action in pursuit of freedom or who seeks the protection of France on other grounds'.

Stemming from an agreement set up between certain States outside of the framework of the European Union, the Schengen system has in stages become integrated into the mechanisms of the Union, although without becoming an integral part of it.

In addition to the five founding States, most of the members of the European Union have joined Schengen, notably Italy in 1990, Spain and Portugal in 1991, and Greece in 1992. In 1997 a protocol annexed to the Treaty of Amsterdam, implemented by two decisions of the Council of 20 May 1999, replaced the Schengen agreements, which thereby became integrated into the law of the European Union. The Regulations of 18 February 2003 (Dublin II)[70] and of 26 June 2013 (Dublin III)[71] in particular determined which Member State is responsible for examining an application for asylum when the asylum seeker applies to several countries in succession.

The Schengen Area nevertheless remains distinct, in part, from that of the territory of the European Union for three reasons. First, four countries of the Union—Cyprus, Bulgaria, Romania, and Croatia—have not, at least at the present time, entered the Schengen system. Second, the United Kingdom and Ireland apply it only partially. Finally, by contrast, four States which remain outside the EU—Norway, Iceland, Switzerland, and Liechtenstein—are parties to Schengen. The vote in February of 2014 by Switzerland in favour of immigration quotas which are enforceable against Union citizens

---

[70] Council Regulation (EC) 343/2003 of 18 February 2003.

[71] Council Regulation (EC) 604/2013 of the European Parliament and of the Council of 26 June 2013.

may, however, compromise the relations of Switzerland with the European Union.

Opening up an area of free movement, the Schengen agreements presuppose border checks on the external frontiers of the area. The application of the Schengen agreements may, in cases of serious security concerns or strong migratory pressure, lead to tensions. Thus the States agreed in 2013, together with the Commission, on the possibility of reestablishing border checks for a period of six months, renewable once, in exceptional circumstances or in the event of uncontrollable immigration pressure.

The Eurozone

Within the framework of the Economic and Monetary Union, eleven countries decided in 1999 to adopt the euro as their common currency. These countries were: Germany, Austria, Belgium, Spain, Finland, France, Ireland, Italy, Luxembourg, the Netherlands, and Portugal. The euro in effect replaced national currencies on 1 January 2002. Eight other members of the Union followed suit: Greece in 2001, Slovenia in 2007, Cyprus and Malta in 2008, Slovakia in 2009, and finally the three Baltic States, Estonia in 2011, Latvia in 2014, and Lithuania in 2015. Nineteen of the twenty-eight Member States of the European Union thus belong to the Eurozone.

The members of the Eurozone are bound by the Stability and Growth Pact, governed initially by two Council Regulations of 7 July 1997.[72] Their monetary policy is determined by the European Central Bank within the framework of the European central banks. The euro group convenes the finance ministers of the Member States.

From 2008 the economic crisis made it necessary for the Member States of the Eurozone temporarily to suspend the rules requiring both

---

[72] Council Regulation (EC) 1466/1997 on the strengthening of the surveillance of budgetary positions and the surveillance and co-ordination of economic policies and Council Regulation (EC) 1467/1997 on speeding up and clarifying the implementation of the excessive deficit procedure.

that each state's deficit must not exceed 3 per cent of its gross domestic product, and that its public debt must not exceed 60 per cent of its gross domestic product. The difficulties connected with the sovereign debt crises—in particular in Ireland, in Greece, in Portugal, and in Spain— led the Member States to look for new mechanisms of regulation, while looking to more integrated economic and budgetary governance.

After the creation in May 2010 of the European Financial Stability Facility, the European Council, relying on the simplified revision procedure set out by the Lisbon Treaty, decided on 25 March 2011 to modify Article 136 of the TFEU with a view to authorizing the Eurozone Member States to institute the European Stability Mechanism, which on 1 July 2012 succeeded the Facility. An international financial institution constituted by the Eurozone countries, the European Stability Mechanism has its seat in Luxembourg.

A treaty of broader application was signed, on 2 March 2012, by twenty-five of the twenty-seven members, after the United Kingdom and the Czech Republic refused to join. Entitled the Treaty on Stability, Coordination and Governance in the Economic and Monetary Union,[73] this treaty, known as the European Fiscal Compact, provides for the adoption of a 'golden rule' which forbids structural deficits above 0.5 per cent of GDP, or 1 per cent for those States whose public debt is below 60 per cent of GDP. The Court of Justice can, if a State brings a case before it, impose sanctions of up to 0.1 per cent of GDP on a State which is alleged to have breached the undertakings set out in the treaty. The treaty institutionalized a regular meeting, at least twice per year, of heads of state and governments of the Eurozone countries. The Conseil constitutionnel, on 9 August 2012,[74] and the German Federal Constitutional Court, on 12 September 2012,[75] determined that neither in France nor in Germany

---

[73] Treaty on Stability, Coordination and Governance in the Economic and Monetary Union, 2 March 2012, not published in the Official Journal.
[74] Decision No 2012–653 of 9 August 2012.   [75] BVerfGE 132, 195.

did the adoption of the treaty breach any constitutional rules. In its judgment in *Pringle*, on 27 November 2012,[76] the Court of Justice of the European Union recognized the treaty's conformity with the law of the Union. Its entry into force, which used a novel mechanism and was dependent on the ratification of twelve Eurozone States, became effective on 1 January 2013.

Sixty years after the signing of the treaty instituting the ECSC, the road travelled towards the construction of Europe is impressive. The difficulties which have punctuated the march have at times stymied progress, but have never stopped it. Still, the course is not without its uncertainties, imperfections, and hesitations. But within a geographic space that has been considerably enlarged, now spanning an entire and indeed reunified continent, the countries of Europe have attained a level of economic and political solidarity that undoubtedly surpasses the hopes of the founding fathers. One of the achievements on which the edifice rests is the emerging European legal order.

---

[76] Case C–370/12 *Pringle* ECLI:EU:C:2012:675.

3

The European Legal Order

I am European; I love the flag which I have worn since my youth.

—Ivan Turgenev

The European project, constructed on the basis of various international treaties, gave precedence from the outset to a series of principles, rules, and courts forming the framework of Community law and of the European Convention on Human Rights.[1] Its creation represented a new and unique legal order.

No traditional classification—whether in terms of defining it as a 'federation' or 'confederation'—quite captures the nature of the project. Europe brings together domestic legal orders which themselves draw upon strong traditions derived from their often long history. Some of these systems are of the common law kind whilst others are Roman-Germanic. Through interpretation, however, they come ever closer together, in a harmonizing and converging dynamic, forming the two principal sources of European law.

On the one hand Community law, now the law of the European Union, has confirmed that, within the framework of the system drawn up by the Treaty of Lisbon,[2] it displays the essence of an integrated and

---

[1] Convention for the Protection of Human Rights and Fundamental Freedoms, 4 November 1950, 213 UNTS 221.

[2] Amending the Treaty on European Union and the Treaty Establishing the European Community, 13 December 2007, [2007] OJ C306/1.

Towards a European Public Law. First Edition. Bernard Stirn. © Bernard Stirn 2017. Published 2017 by Oxford University Press.

clearly affirmed legal order.[3] Alongside the European Union a Europe of human rights continues to develop,[4] on the basis of the European Convention on Human Rights, interpreted and implemented with dynamism by the European Court of Human Rights. What emerges from the confluence of the law of the European Union and of the European Convention is a European legal order worthy of the name.

1. THE EUROPEAN UNION AFTER THE LISBON TREATY

Together making up the Treaty of Lisbon, the Treaty on European Union (TEU) and the Treaty on the Functioning of the European Union (TFEU) give the European Union legal order its principles and its values, its institutional organization, and its normative system.

The Principles and Values of the European Union

According to the preamble introducing it, the Treaty on European Union was concluded:

> DRAWING INSPIRATION from the cultural, religious and humanist inheritance of Europe, from which have developed the universal values of the inviolable and inalienable rights of the human person, freedom, democracy, equality and the rule of law.

Carefully balanced, with a view to affirming a spiritual heritage whilst aiming to be neutral with regard to religion and allowing for freedom of conscience and belief, this provision sets out the values which are then developed in more legal terms in Article 2:

---

[3] See P Craig, *The Lisbon Treaty: Law, Politics, and Treaty Reform* (OUP 2010).
[4] See H Keller and A Stone Sweet, *A Europe of Rights: The Impact of the ECHR on National Legal Systems* (OUP 2008).

The Union is founded on the values of respect for human dignity, freedom, democracy, equality, the rule of law and respect for human rights, including the rights of persons belonging to minorities. These values are common to the Member States in a society in which pluralism, non-discrimination, tolerance, justice, solidarity and equality between women and men prevail.

Since its very beginnings, the European Union has been more than just a commercial space founded upon free movement and an openness towards competition. The European Union is a democratic space, based on certain political values. It is devoted to the safeguarding of fundamental rights, in keeping with Article 6 of the Treaty, and is established as an organized democracy, according to the conditions set out by Article 10.

Article 6 of the Treaty provides that the Union recognizes 'the rights, freedoms and principles set out in the Charter of Fundamental Rights of the European Union of 7 December 2000, as adapted at Strasbourg, on 12 December 2007' and conferred on the Charter 'the same legal value as the Treaties'. It envisages the accession of the European Union to the European Convention on Human Rights, though the way in which this will happen remains unclear. Consolidating the jurisprudence of the Court of Justice, it sets out that:

[f]undamental rights, as guaranteed by the European Convention for the Protection of Human Rights and Fundamental Freedoms and as they result from the constitutional traditions common to the Member States, shall constitute general principles of the Union's law.

According to Article 10 '[t]he functioning of the Union shall be founded on representative democracy'. That democratic representation is organized on the one hand directly, through the election of the European Parliament by citizens, on the other hand indirectly, through the presence of the heads of state and government within the

European Council and of ministers in the Council; all these authorities are 'themselves democratically accountable either to their national Parliaments, or to their citizens'. Every citizen has 'the right to participate in the democratic life of the Union'. Furthermore, a 'European citizens' initiative' was set up. Having come into force on 1 April 2012, it gives to a million individuals from at least a quarter of the Member States the right to present to the Commission their project. Since 2012 three initiatives, relating to the rights to water, the protection of the embryo, and the fight against experiments on animals, have met the threshold. Political parties at European level are noted as contributing 'to forming European political awareness and to expressing the will of citizens of the Union'.

Respecting the rights and fundamental principles set out in the Treaty is a necessary condition in order to become a member of the European Union. A procedure is in place for the scenario in which a State breaches these rights and principles. With a majority of four-fifths of its members and after obtaining the consent of the European Parliament, the Council can decide, in accordance with Article 7 of the Treaty, 'that there is a clear risk of a serious breach by a Member State of the values' set out in Article 2. If the State is guilty of a serious and persistent breach of those values, the procedure may lead to the suspension of the rights the State enjoys by virtue of the Treaty.

After Hungary adopted a new constitution in April 2011, the European Commission envisaged bringing a case before the Court of Justice, as it worried that the principles set out above might have been breached, along with further concerns as to the independence of the judiciary, the independence of the Central Bank, and the Data Protection Authority. Although the Commission eventually struck a compromise with the government of Viktor Orbán, tensions have nevertheless from time to time reappeared between Hungary and the Commission. An example are the events of the spring of 2015, in the wake of declarations made by the Head of the Hungarian government advocating an end to immigration in the country and evoking the possibility of reinstating the death penalty. In the summer of 2012, worries as to the respect for the democratic requirements of the Union arose in connection with Romania, as the Romanian government tried to depose President Traian Băsescu. As a result of participation levels being too low (46 per cent), the referendum organized on 29 July 2012 permitted him to stay, but uncertainties have lingered as to the independence of the Constitutional Court. These two examples show that the full extent of democratic principles is not comprehensively consolidated throughout the entirety of the European Union.

The Institutional Organization

Although the Treaty of Lisbon preserves the institutional characteristics of a system which has progressively taken shape around the European Council, the Council, the Commission, the European Parliament, and the Court of Justice, the Treaty also profoundly renews the rules which determine the configuration and competences of these great organizations upon which the Union rests. It also determines the competences of other institutions and bodies which, although not enjoying as important a place in the greater edifice, nevertheless play a complementary role within it.

The European Council

In the first meeting of the heads of state or of government which took place in 1974, at the instigation of President Giscard d'Estaing and Chancellor Helmut Schmidt, the European Council was not mentioned in the Treaties until the Single Act[5] and the Treaty of Maastricht.[6] With the Lisbon Treaty, the European Council became an institution of the Union. The Treaty furthermore gives it a stable presidency: the European Council elects its president by qualified majority for a duration of two and a half years, renewable once. The president of the European Council may not exercise responsibilities

[5] Bulletin of the European Communities, No 6/1987 at [2.4.5].
[6] Treaty on European Union, 7 February 1992, 1757 UNTS 3, [1992] OJ C224/1.

in his or her home state simultaneously. The former Belgian Prime Minister, Herman Van Rompuy, was the first to exercise these functions, from 1 December 2009. After he had finished two mandates, the Polish Prime Minister, Donald Tusk, succeeded him on 1 December 2014.

The European Council is composed of heads of state or governments of the Member States, as well as its president and the president of the Commission. The High Representative of the Union for Foreign Affairs and Security Policy, another function created by the Lisbon Treaty, assists in its proceedings. The High Representative is at the same time the Vice President of the Commission. The functions of High Representative were performed first by Baroness Ashton and then, from 2014, by the former Italian Foreign Minister, Federica Mogherini.

Meeting at least four times per year, the European Council 'shall provide the Union with the necessary impetus for its development and shall define the general political directions and priorities thereof'.[7] It makes pronouncements on the basis of consensus.

The Council

Fulfilling its functions within the framework set out by the European Council, the Council is an executive organ consisting of representatives with minister status from every State. Its composition varies as a function of its agenda: in particular it convokes, according to the subjects to be dealt with, the foreign ministers, the ministers of finance, the ministers of agriculture, or the transport ministers. The TEU specifically mentions the composition of the Council as a General Affairs Council, which convenes the ministers of foreign affairs and which is tasked with assuring the coherence of the various Council configurations as well as preparing the meetings of the European Council whilst ensuring the follow-up meetings together with the president of the European Council and the Commission.

[7] Art 15 TEU.

The presidency of the Council is held by the minister of one of the States, according to the concept of equal rotation, every six months. The Council of foreign affairs, which brings together the ministers of foreign affairs, is however presided over by the High Representative of the Union for Foreign Affairs and Security Policy. The work of the Council is prepared by the Committee of Permanent Representatives, that is, the ambassadors of every State Member within the European Union.

Since the Lisbon Treaty came into force, the Council will, unless there are treaty provisions to the contrary, take its decisions by qualified majority, defined on the basis of a weighting of votes between Member States, in line with their population. According to the rules applicable since 1 November 2014, of a total of 352 votes, Germany, France, the United Kingdom, and Italy each dispose of twenty-nine, Spain and Poland of twenty-seven, whereas, amongst the States with fewer inhabitants, Latvia, Slovenia, Estonia, Cyprus, and Luxembourg have four and Malta three. In order to be adopted, a decision must be taken by at least fifteen States (or 55 per cent of the States) and receive 260 votes (which represents 65 per cent of the population). A blocking minority of ninety-three votes may furthermore oppose a decision.

The Commission

As one of the original institutions, the Commission has been viewed since it was founded as a collegiate body, tasked to incarnate and defend, beyond national particularisms, the general interest as set out by the Treaties. It played an important role in the evolution of the European construct, in particular under the presidencies of first Walter Hallstein (1958–67); then of Jacques Delors, from the era of the establishment of the internal market and the institutional changes (1985–95); and more recently of Romano Prodi (1999–2004). After José Manuel Barroso, former head of the Portuguese government, who presided over the Commission in 2004–14, came the former Prime Minister of Luxembourg, Jean-Claude Juncker.

Article 17 of the TEU defines the mission of the Commission along the lines of a continuity of its history:

> The Commission shall promote the general interest of the Union and take appropriate initiatives to that end. It shall ensure the application of the Treaties, and of measures adopted by the institutions pursuant to the Treaties.... In carrying out its responsibilities, the Commission shall be completely independent.

The mandate of the Commission lasts for five years. Its president is elected by the European Parliament, by a majority of the members of which it is composed. The European Council, acting by a qualified majority, first proposes a candidate to the Parliament and the process must be done by '[t]aking into account the elections to the European Parliament'.[8] Thus the president designates and the Council determines together the list of commissioners, chosen, on the suggestion of the Member States, 'on the ground of their general competence and European commitment from persons whose independence is beyond doubt'.[9] The college is then presented to the Parliament for approbation and then nominated by the European Council by qualified majority.

The Commission is responsible to the European Parliament, which can put an end to its operation by voting through a motion of censure. Such a motion has never been voted through; but in 1999 the Commission presided over by the Luxembourgeois Jacques Santer resigned in the face of the prospect of the Parliament adopting such a motion in respect of him.

The Treaty of Lisbon provides that the Commission shall have a commissioner per Member State. It also opens up the possibility that it be composed, after a unanimous decision by the Council, of a number of members corresponding to two-thirds of the number of Member States. In that case, a rotation is organized, corresponding

---

[8] Art 17(7) TEU.   [9] Art 17(3) TEU.

to a system which reflects 'the demographic and geographic range of all the Member States'.[10] The Commission exercises three powers: a power of initiative, of execution, and of sanction. Unless an exception is provided for by the Treaties, the Commission has a monopoly of initiative in connection with the adoption of regulations and directives. On the authorization of the Council, the Commission takes the measures necessary for the application of secondary Union law, most often after having had the view of a committee with special competence in the matter in question, according to the rules of 'comitology'.

Charged with the application of the Treaties, the Commission has a power of sanction with regard to the enterprises which do not respect the principle of free competition and may initiate infringement procedures or actions for failure to act against Members States, following a complaint or of its own initiative.

As for the exercise of its functions, the Commission is supported by significant administrative services, structured in Directorates-General. It employs 38,000 European civil servants, recruited through centrally organized exams, conducted with a view to securing a balanced representation of the different nationalities of the Union.

The European Parliament

Elected for five years, by direct universal suffrage since 1979, the European Parliament consists, following the Lisbon Treaty, of 751 deputies. Any one State may not have more than ninety-six seats (Germany) nor fewer than six (Estonia, Cyprus, Luxembourg, and Malta). France elects seventy-four deputies; the United Kingdom and Italy, seventy-three.

The competences of the European Parliament have progressively enlarged with a view to achieving, on the basis of the Lisbon Treaty, the extension of co-decision, now characterized as 'the ordinary

---

[10] Art 17(5) TEU.

legislative procedure', with the Council, in budgetary as well as legislative matters. With the election of the president of the Commission
and his or her responsibility before the latter, the European Parliament
possesses prerogatives of political control, making it similar to
national parliaments.

Its members are divided in seven political groups, of which the two
most important are the European People's Party, close to Christian
Democracy, and the Progressive Alliance of Socialists and Democrats,
which draws inspiration from Social Democracy. Its President, the
German Social Democrat Martin Schultz, elected in 2012, was re-
elected in 2014 following an agreement between the two groups.

With complex electoral systems, particular to each State, elections for
the European Parliament nevertheless do not mobilize the populations
sufficiently: the participation rate, which rose to 63 per cent at the first
election held in 1979 on the basis of universal suffrage, was no higher
than 43 per cent in 2014. In certain new Member States participation
even fell well short of this average, being no higher than 23 per cent in
Poland, 21 per cent in the Czech Republic, and 13 per cent in Slovakia.

The Court of Justice of the European Union

A real European judicial order has come into being over time. After
the entry into force of the Lisbon Treaty, this judicial order consists of
(under the new name the Court of Justice of the European Union) the
Court of Justice, the General Court, and the Civil Service Tribunal.
The litigation before these three courts of law is voluminous and
growing. All three courts do their best to deal with this case-load and
to reduce the time it takes them to hand down their judgments. As
a result of the rulings of these three courts, the law of the European
Union has a strong case-law dimension.

The Court of Justice is composed of one judge per State and eleven
Advocates General,[11] appointed for a renewable mandate of six years.

---

[11] According to the Decision of the Council of 25 June 2013, the number of
Advocates General was raised from eight to nine on 1 July 2013; from 7 October 2015
the number is eleven.

The judges elect from amongst themselves a president for a three-year term. From 2003 to 2015, the Court of Justice was presided over by Vassilios Skouris, of Greek nationality; its current president is the Belgian Koen Lenaerts. The judges and Advocates General are assisted by référendaires,[12] chosen by themselves. They also have other highly qualified assistants, allowing them to study in depth the cases filed before the Court.

The role played by the Advocate General is comparable to that of the *rapporteur public* in French administrative courts: according to Article 252 of the TFEU, he or she has the duty, 'acting with complete impartiality and independence, to make, in open court, reasoned submissions on cases'. If a case does not present any new legal questions, the Court may, however, pronounce on it without the assistance of the conclusions of the Advocate General.

About half of the cases are decided according to this modified procedure. There is a convention according to which Germany, France, Italy, the United Kingdom, Spain, and now also Poland should always be represented amongst the Advocates General.

Judges and Advocates General are nominated by common agreement by the governments of the Member States, 'from persons whose independence is beyond doubt and who possess the qualifications required for appointment to the highest judicial offices in their respective countries or who are jurisconsults of recognised competence'.[13] Article 255 of the TFEU instituted a committee of seven members, made up of former members of the Court of Justice or of the General Court, members of national supreme courts, and lawyers of recognized competence, 'to give an opinion on candidates' suitability to perform the duties of Judge and Advocate-General of the Court of Justice and the General Court'. The Vice President of the French Conseil d'État, Jean-Marc Sauvé, chairs the committee. Lord Mance

---

[12] Référendaires are legal secretaries, who assist the judges and the Advocates General of the Court; they research case-law and may assist with the drafting of a judgment or an opinion.

[13] Art 19(2) TEU.

of the UK Supreme Court is also a member. By involving national supreme courts in the choice of the judges of the Union, the committee exemplifies the ties between national and European judges. Its decisions have always been followed by the States, which have systematically withdrawn the candidatures which have met with an unfavourable view on the part of the panel.

The Court pronounces on two types of case. On the one hand, questions to be settled by way of preliminary rulings either regarding the interpretation of the treaties or the validity and interpretation of acts of the institutions, bodies, offices, or agencies of the Union are referred to it, by the courts of the Member States. According to Article 267 of the TFEU, such questions can be referred to it by any court of a Member State. For domestic supreme courts, bringing such a matter before the Court of Justice is obligatory.

On the other hand, the Court of Justice hears cases of annulment or failure to act, brought by a Member State or an institution of the Union against an institution or a State. If the Court concludes that a State has failed to live up to its obligation to transpose a directive, it may decide that the State has to pay a lump-sum fine or a penalty for delay.

In addition to these competences, the Court of Justice sits in cases directed against the decisions of the General Court.

The Court of Justice delivers its rulings in Chambers of three to five judges or in a Grand Chamber consisting of fifteen judges. Cases which do not present any difficulties may be dealt with by way of orders.[14] The Court may examine certain cases according to an accelerated procedure and even, in respect of prejudicial questions, according to an urgency procedure, which allows it to make a pronouncement within approximately two months.

With the preliminary ruling procedure, the law of the European Union gives an organized framework to the concept of judicial dialogue.

---

[14] These orders are summary judicial decisions, rather than refusals of permission to bring a case to the Court, as in English judicial review procedure.

In terms of that judicial dialogue, certain tensions arose at the outset, in particular when the French Conseil d'État, applying its traditional jurisprudence, decided that, even so far as the top French courts were concerned, the preliminary ruling procedure could be used only in cases of serious difficulty.[15] However, the Court of Justice itself adopted a similar position, by affirming that the domestic courts should not bring a matter before it in cases where the Court had already made a pronouncement or if 'the correct application of Community law is so obvious as to leave no scope for any reasonable doubt'.[16]

Regularly resorted to by the domestic courts, in particular the highest courts, the preliminary ruling procedure forges close bonds between the domestic courts and the Court of Justice. The judgments rendered by the latter in the context of preliminary rulings clarify the law not only for that country whose court has brought the matter before the Court of Justice, but also for the whole Union. The Conseil d'État, which by now participates fully in the preliminary rulings procedure, recognizes that the authority of the judgments of the Court of Justice in this connection is binding on all, beyond the particular case of the State that brought the matter before the Court.[17]

The creation of the General Court and the Civil Service Tribunal enabled delays in the Court's case management to be reduced. In 2014 a total of 622 cases were referred to it (of which 428 were preliminary references, seventy-four cases brought directly before the Court, and 111 against decisions of the General Court) and rendered judgment in 719 of them. The number of pending cases was 787 on 1 January 2015. The Court has regularly reduced this number over the last few years, with a view to bringing it down to the equivalent of the annual capacity of judgment. As regards preliminary references, the average time the Court takes to process a case was (in 2014) approximately fifteen months. In 2014, the Court examined

---

[15] Conseil d'État, 19 June 1964, *Société des pétroles Shell-Berre.*
[16] Case C–283/81 *CILFIT* ECLI:EU:C:1982:335.
[17] Conseil d'État, 11 December 2006, *Société De Groot.*

ten of the preliminary references according to its accelerated procedure and four according to its urgency procedure.

The General Court was created in 1988, as the Court of First Instance, in order to relieve the Court of Justice, particularly with respect to cases concerning competition law, state aid, and intellectual property. With the Treaty of Lisbon, it took the name 'General Court of the European Union' and became the court of first resort for all of the general law of the EU. It is composed of at least one judge per State, but it does not have Advocates General. Its decisions may, in respect of legal questions, be appealed to the Court of Justice.

The General Court sits in cases of actions for annulment, failure to act, and failure to fulfil an obligation (which are not the sole domain of the Court) and actions for damages directed against the Union. Its competences especially concern competition and mergers, state aid, patents, and trademarks. Cases may also be brought before it on questions of law, seeking appeal to judgments of the Civil Service Tribunal.

In 2014 the General Court sat in 912 cases, of which 423 were annulment proceedings and thirty-six were appeals against decisions of the Civil Service Tribunal. A total of 295 cases concerned intellectual property; 148, state aid. The same year the General Court handed down 814 decisions. Its pending case-load is about 1,400 cases, which translates to up to an average of twenty-four months to process a case.

Confronted with a growing case-load and demanding cases, the General Court has struggled to match up the in- and out-going cases. Thus it envisages doubling, in three successive stages, its number of members from now until 2019. That would, in return, allow it to absorb the Civil Service Tribunal.

Created in 2004, the Civil Service Tribunal is composed of seven judges nominated for six years by the Council, on the advice of a committee made up of former judges of the Court or of the General Court and lawyers of recognized competence. It decides, in the first place, all of the cases related to the civil service of the European Union.

In 2014 the Civil Service Tribunal received 157 cases and rendered a decision in 152. As at 1 January 2015 its current case-load was 216; the average time to process a case was around thirteen months.

Other specialist courts may be instituted by the Council. Thus a patent court for example has been envisaged. However, at present it seems more likely that the General Court will be strengthened rather than cases being directed to specialist tribunals.

Complementary Organs and Institutions

Amongst the institutions of the European Union, there are also the European Central Bank and the European Court of Auditors. The Treaty of Lisbon adds that the Parliament, the Council, and the Commission are 'assisted by an Economic and Social Committee and a Committee of the Regions, exercising advisory functions'. Finally, it also brings into existence a European Ombudsman.

Created in the wake of the Maastricht Treaty, the European Central Bank, based in Frankfurt, became an institution of the European Union with the adoption of the Lisbon Treaty. A European network of central banks, bringing together the central banks of the twenty-seven Member States, has sprung up around it; so has the Eurosystem, which brings together the nineteen countries of the Eurozone.[18]

The European Central Bank is in charge of the Union's monetary policy, which is, for the countries that have adopted the euro, an exclusive competence of the Union. It is directed by a council of the governors of the central banks and by an Executive Board of six members (including the president) who are appointed for a mandate of eight non-renewable years by the European Council. This is done by qualified majority voting, on the recommendation of the Council and after consultation with the European Parliament and the council of governors. The Executive Board has been presided over by the Dutchman Wim Duisenberg, from its inception in 1998 until 2003, by the former governor of the Banque de France, Jean-Claude Trichet, from 2003 until 2011, and then, from November 2011, by Mario Draghi. With its assertive independence and authority, the European Central Bank comes close to being a federal institution.

---

[18] Austria, Belgium, Cyprus, Estonia, Finland, France, Germany, Greece, Ireland, Italy, Latvia, Lithuania, Luxembourg, Malta, the Netherlands, Portugal, Slovakia, Slovenia, and Spain.

Created by the Treaty of 22 July 1975, which reinforced the budgetary powers of the European Parliament, the Court of Auditors became a Union institution through the Treaty of Maastricht. It is made up by one member per State, proposed by each State and nominated for six years, renewable by the Council on qualified majority voting, after consultation with the European Parliament. The members of the Court elect their president for three renewable years. The Court audits all of the European Union's finances and acts to assure good financial governance. Its powers of investigation are large and it may, in a wide-ranging manner, produce reports and opinions. It draws up an annual public report. In this way, although it does not have powers of sanction, it has a useful role to play in the husbandry of the funds of the Union.

The European Economic and Social Committee and the Committee of the Regions are purely consultative bodies. Set up by the two Treaties of Rome of 1957,[19] the Economic and Social Committee has a maximum of 350 members, nominated for five years by the Council, on the basis of suggestions made by the States and according to an agreed allocation between them. Its function is to represent the economic and social actors of civil society; this fits particularly well with an Italian and French tradition of corporatism, which is not found in the United Kingdom. Similar rules of appointment apply to the Committee of the Regions, created by the Treaty of Maastricht. It too is made up of a maximum of 350 members, representing the regions and other local authorities.

Set up by the Treaty of Maastricht as part of the idea of European citizenship, the European Ombudsman is appointed for five non-renewable years by the European Parliament. Whether on his or her own initiative or by reason of a complaint, he or she investigates all types of cases of bad administration on the part of the Union institutions (with the exception of the Court of Justice in its exercise of its

---

[19] Treaty Establishing the European Economic Community, 25 March 1957, 298 UNTS 3.

judicial functions). He or she draws up recommendations and every year submits a report to the European Parliament.

Initiated on the basis of the Schengen Agreement[20] within an inter-governmental framework, co-operation in criminal matters took on an EU dimension with the adoption of the Treaty of Amsterdam.[21]

Two agencies—Europol and Eurojust—carry out the functions of this legal co-operation. Conceived in the image of Interpol, Europol has since 1999 affected exchanges and analyses of information with a view to prevent and suppress organized crime.

Eurojust, set up in 2002, facilitates mutual assistance in criminal matters between Member States. A new dimension was opened up in this connection by Article 86 of the TFEU, providing that, having obtained the consent of the European Parliament, the Council acting unanimously, or a group of at least nine States, may decide to create a European Public Prosecutor's Office, which would be competent to combat offences against the Union's financial interests and, when appropriate, serious cross-border crime. A report into the subject was produced in 2011 by the Conseil d'État for the French government.[22] Proposed in 2013 by the Commission and approved in 2014 by the European Parliament, the legislative proposal setting up the European Public Prosecutor's Office is being deliberated in the Council. The fight against terrorism adds a supplementary justification for its creation.

The System of Rules of the European Union

In addition to the Treaties, which make up the primary sources of law, or primary legislation, the European Union's system of rules has the

---

[20] Agreement between the States of the Benelux Economic Union, Germany and France on the Gradual Abolition of Checks at their Common Frontiers, [2000] OJ L239/13.

[21] Amending the TEU, the Treaties Establishing the European Communities and Certain Related Acts, [1997] OJ C340/1.

[22] Réflexions sur l'institution d'un parquet européen (Conseil d'État 2011).

great originality of also possessing sources of secondary law, secondary legislation, encompassing the rules adopted by the Union institutions by virtue of the Treaties.

Secondary Legislation

Signed, ratified, and published by each Member State according to its own constitutional requirements, the constitutive Treaties and their successive modifications, follow, as far as the methods of their adoption and their entry into force are concerned, the classic rules of public international law.[23] However, they confer on the institutions which they have created certain normative competences, by virtue of which these institutions decree sources of secondary law, which themselves enter into force on their publication in the Official Journal of the European Union, without the intervention of the Member States.

Reproducing the rules which could be found in Article 189 of the Treaty of Rome from the outset, Article 288 of the TFEU, concerning the legal acts of the Union, defines the sources of secondary law as being regulations, directives, and decisions.

'A regulation shall have general application. It shall be binding in its entirety and directly applicable in all Member States.'[24] A regulation thus applies both to States and to individuals. Its provisions do not necessitate national measures of execution; it has full direct effect, in the sense that it applies as between individuals (horizontal effect), upwards as between individuals and the State (ascending vertical effect), and downwards as between the State and individuals (descending vertical effect). The Court of Justice has observed that 'by reason of their nature and their function in the system of sources of Community Law, regulations have direct effect and are, as such, capable of creating individual rights which national courts must protect.'[25]

---

[23] See especially the Vienna Convention on the Law of Treaties, 23 May 1969, 1155 UNTS 331; Sir Frank Berman and E Bjorge, 'Treaties' in Sir Christopher Greenwood and D Sarooshi (eds), *Oppenheim's International Law* (10th edn, OUP 2017); Lord McNair, *The Law of Treaties* (2nd edn, OUP 1961).
[24] Art 288 TFEU.   [25] Case 43–71 *Politi* ECLI:EU:C:1971:122.

'A directive shall be binding, as to the result to be achieved, upon each Member State to which it is addressed, but shall leave to the national authorities the choice of form and methods.'[26] Setting aims and objectives, a directive implies that the Member States adopt measures to transpose it, in respect of which the States have a measure of latitude. There is a time limit for the transposition of each directive.

'A decision shall be binding in its entirety. A decision which specifies those to whom it is addressed shall be binding only on them.'[27] Having direct effect, in the same way as regulations, a decision has an ambit that goes no further than those companies or individuals which it sets out to cover.

Regulations, directives, and decisions must all be reasoned; their premises must be set out.

Furthermore, the Union may conclude, both with a third State and with other international organizations, international treaties which bind Member States.[28]

For the issuance of secondary legislation, the Commission has the power of initiative and monopoly on legislative proposition. Regulations and directives, referred to by the Lisbon Treaty as 'legislative acts' (Article 48), are in principle adopted in accordance with the 'ordinary legislative procedure' by the Parliament and the Council and by the means of qualified majority voting.

A 'special legislative procedure' applies in the situations where the Council acts by unanimity or where the Parliament has only limited powers. Legislative acts are distinct from 'delegated acts', the adoption of which may be delegated to the Commission by a legislative act, and 'implementing acts', which by their nature come under the Commission.

The importance of secondary legislation is considerable. A total of 8,400 regulations and close to 2,000 directives are in force. Every year around 200 regulations and sixty directives are adopted, covering an

---

[26] Art 288 TFEU.   [27] ibid.
[28] See eg P Eeckhout, *EU External Relations Law* (2nd edn, OUP 2011).

increasingly broad array of subjects. The European Union is further-more bound by 3,000 international treaties concluded by it. With a view to strengthening legal certainty, the Commission aims to check what has been termed 'normative inflation'. On the heels of the 'better regulation' objective of the Barroso Commission, the Juncker Commission has been committed, as a matter of improving regulation, to establish a long-term programme of joint adoption of rules by the Council and the Parliament.

In addition to these rules come numerous elements of soft law. Opinions and recommendations, as set out in the TFEU, are without binding force but not without any legal effect, as domestic courts must take them into account in the contexts within which they apply.[29] For instance, Communications; Green Papers, serving to launch debates; White Papers, drawing conclusions from such debates; resolutions; and reports are more informal.

The Commission supervises the States' faithful application of secondary legislation. It acts on its own initiative or at the suit of an enterprise or an individual. After a dialogue phase, it may serve on the State in question a letter of formal notice and then a reasoned opinion. If this pre-litigation stage does not lead anywhere, the Commission may seise the Court of Justice, which has the power to impose on the defaulting State the payment of a lump sum or a penalty payment. The number of infringement procedures is ever-decreasing, having gone from 3,400 in 2007 to 761 in 2013 and this is a result of the increasingly faithful application of EU law by the Member States. Almost 90 per cent of the procedures are closed before it becomes necessary to refer the matter to the Court of Justice.

The Authority of Directives

The distinction drawn by the wording of the Treaty of Rome between regulations and directives could lead one to think that a directive does not have any effect in the law of a Member State until the latter has

---

[29] Case C–322/88 *Grimaldi* ECLI:EU:C:1989:646.

taken the necessary measures to transpose it into domestic law. The Court of Justice, however, developed a body of case-law according to which even a non-transposed directive will, if it is sufficiently precise, be directly applicable in the Member States.[30] This position is explained both by the concern to encourage the State to transpose directives and by the realization that directives are, relatively often, drafted in a way that leaves little by way of latitude to the domestic authorities in terms of the determination of the methods of their application.

The incremental adoption of this jurisprudence by domestic courts did not come about without difficulty. In Italy, the Consiglio di Stato[31] and the Corte di cassazione[32] at first refused to recognize the direct effect of directives. In Germany, the Federal Fiscal Court adopted the same view, until the Federal Constitutional Court at Karlsruhe took issue with the Federal Fiscal Court's approach and rallied behind the jurisprudence of the Court of Justice. This was not, however, without noting that the former had not gone beyond the limits of a transfer of sovereignty on the part of Germany.[33]

It is, however, in France where the conflict has been the most animated and where the courts took the longest to fall into line. At the suit of the political activist Daniel Cohn-Bendit, the Conseil d'État was, in 1978, seised of a question regarding the Directive of 25 February 1964 concerning restrictions of free movement on the grounds of public order:[34] had the decision taken ten years earlier, in the wake of the events of May 1968, to refuse to repeal Mr Cohn-Bendit's expulsion order been legal? The *Commissaire du gouvernement*, Bruno Genevois proposed to support the preliminary reference

---

[30] Case 33–70 *SACE* ECLI:EU:C:1970:118; Case 41–74 *van Duyn* ECLI:EU:C: 1974:133.

[31] Consiglio di Stato, 5 May 1980, *Helen Curtis*.

[32] Corte di cassazione, 7 October 1981, *Ministry of Finance v Cartiere Timavo*.

[33] Federal Constitutional Court, Judgment of 8 April 1987.

[34] Council Directive 64/221/EEC of 25 February 1964 on the co-ordination of special measures concerning the movement and residence of foreign nationals which are justified on grounds of public policy, public security or public health.

that the Administrative Tribunal of Paris had wanted to make, by way of inviting the Conseil d'État to re-examine, if it deemed it necessary, its jurisprudence, all the while keeping in mind the wording of the Treaty. He observed: 'At the level of the European Community, there ought not to be government of judges, nor war of judges. There ought to be room for the dialogue of judges'.

Whilst the sally made its mark,[35] the Conseil d'État did not in the event follow Genevois' conclusions. With reference to the letter of the Treaty, the Conseil d'État decided, on 22 December 1978,[36] that it was clear that a non-transposed directive did not produce any effects in relation to individual decisions and that, for this reason, there was no need to make a preliminary reference.

Incremental developments alleviated the conflict that followed in the wake of this jurisprudence, and then removed it entirely.

Aware of how its jurisprudence had rankled not only in France but also in Italy and Germany, the Court of Justice refined its case-law in two ways. This would have the effect of serving to nuance its approach, whilst showing its desire primarily to encourage the State to transpose Community directives into domestic law. First, a directive produces effects only after the expiration of the deadline for its transposition.[37] Secondly, the direct effect is limited to relations between individuals and the State. In the absence of a measure of transposition, a directive does not have horizontal direct effect between individuals. It may be invoked only, by way of ascending vertical effect, vis-à-vis a State that has failed its obligation of transposition; the State is unable to rely, as against its own citizens, on descending vertical effect.[38]

For its part the Conseil d'État has given directives an increasing authority in domestic law.

---

[35] See now eg F Sudre, 'Du "dialogue des juges" à l'euro-compatibilité' in *Le Dialogue des Juges: Mélanges en l'Honneur du Président Bruno Genevois* (Dalloz 2009) 1028.

[36] Conseil d'État, 22 December 1978, *Ministre de l'intérieur c/ Cohn-Bendit*.

[37] Case 148/78 *Ratti* ECLI:EU:C:1979:110.

[38] Case 152/84 *Marshall* ECLI:EU:C:1986:84; Joined Cases 372–375/85 *Traen and Others* ECLI:EU:C:1987:222.

It decided in an initial phase that a regulation must conform with the trend of a directive, even if the regulation in question did not transpose the directive.[39] In the same vein the Conseil d'État held that not only must a regulation be in conformity with the trend of a directive: a directive was also held to be a new fact (in French '*une circonstance de droit nouvelle*') that would necessitate the modification or abrogation of previous regulations the provisions of which did not conform with the later directive.[40] Finally, the Conseil d'État determined that it was incumbent on State authorities to cease to apply, at the time of the deadline for transposition of the directive, both written and non-written rules of municipal law which are incompatible with the trend of a directive, whether the latter has or has not been transposed.[41] Against this background, the remaining authority of the *Cohn-Bendit* jurisprudence was all but nugatory.

Such conflict which may have lingered was definitively expunged by the 2009 decision *Madame Perreux*.[42] The Conseil d'État in this judgment explained and synthesized its jurisprudence, according to which domestic authorities may not allow regulations to subsist which are incompatible with a directive whose deadline for transposition has expired, nor apply such regulations. The Conseil d'État took its stand both on the constitutional obligation of transposition of directives, an obligation set out by the Conseil constitutionnel on the basis of Article 88-1 of the Constitution,[43] and on the requirements flowing from EU law. On that basis it proceeded

---

[39] Conseil d'État, 7 December 1984, *Fédération française des sociétés de protection de la nature*.

[40] Conseil d'État, 3 February 1989, *Compagnie Alitalia*.

[41] Conseil d'État, 6 February 1998, *Tête*; 20 May 1998, *Communauté de communes du Piémont de Barr*.

[42] Conseil d'État, 30 October 2009, *Madame Perreux*.

[43] Art 88-1 of the French Constitution (now) provides: 'The Republic shall participate in the European Union constituted by States which have freely chosen to exercise some of their powers in common by virtue of the Treaty on European Union and of the Treaty on the Functioning of the European Union, as they result from the treaty signed in Lisbon on 13 December, 2007.'

to abandon what subsisted of the *Cohn-Bendit* jurisprudence, applying faithfully the jurisprudence of the Court of Justice, by holding that every individual may, in a suit directed against a non-regulatory administrative decision, rely on the provisions of a directive, even a non-transposed one, given that the deadline for transposition is passed and the provisions at issue are precise and unconditional.

On the last point, the *rapporteur public*, Mattias Guyomar, observed that other European supreme courts had already fallen into line, especially the German Federal Constitutional Court,[44] the House of Lords,[45] the Spanish Constitutional Court,[46] and the Belgian Cour de cassation.[47] In France, even the Cour de cassation had taken this step.[48] Guyomar strongly encouraged the Conseil d'État not to continue the course of the outlier, stating that: 'There exist splendid isolations; others are risible. Yours defies both descriptions. But it is at the very least troubling'. The dialogue of judges won the day, assuring legal consistency.

For all Member States, domestic law is thus more and more to be understood within the framework of the law of the European Union, which is completed by the requirements of the 'Europe of human rights'.

2. A EUROPE OF HUMAN RIGHTS

One might have been forgiven for thinking that the European Convention on Human Rights, which essentially reaffirms principles long since recognized by the great European democracies, would, at least in the first instance, have no more than a relatively limited

---

[44] German Federal Constitutional Court, 8 April 1987.
[45] *Foster and Others v British Gas Plc* [1991] 2 AC 306 (Lord Templeman).
[46] Spanish Constitutional Tribunal, 13 July 1991.
[47] Belgian Cour de cassation, 5 December 1994.
[48] Cour de cassation, 23 November 2004.

impact.[49] It was, at all events, difficult to imagine that it would quicken the protection of human rights in Europe in quite the way it has done and that it would exercise the considerable influence on domestic law that it has come to do.

But the evolutionary and progressive jurisprudence of the European Court of Human Rights,[50] the role of which has been gradually asserted to the point that it is now quite extensive, has given rise to a solid system of collective protection of fundamental rights, which has become one of the key components of the European legal order.

For all the constitutional and supreme courts of Europe, the jurisprudence of the Strasbourg Court constitutes an increasingly important point of reference. Setting out a doctrine of considerable importance, Lord Bingham in his speech in the House of Lords judgment in *Ullah*, observed that: 'The duty of national courts is to keep pace with the Strasbourg jurisprudence as it evolves over time: no more but certainly no less.'[51] As this approach has developed over time, there is now room for domestic courts to go beyond, but they must not fall short of the standards set out by the Strasbourg Court.[52]

The Supreme Court of the United Kingdom has taken inspiration from this doctrine, though at times it has gone beyond it. Thus it has held,[53] on the basis of the right to life guaranteed by Article 2 of the Convention, that the positive duty imposed by Article 2 on States to take preventative operational measures to safeguard an individual's life was owed to a mentally ill patient who had voluntarily been

---

[49] See for the backstory H Lauterpacht, *An International Bill of the Rights of Man* (Columbia University Press 1945); reissued with a foreword by P Sands (OUP 2013).

[50] See eg E Bjorge, *The Evolutionary Interpretation of Treaties* (OUP 2014) 10–14.

[51] *R (Ullah) v Special Adjudicator* [2004] UKHL 26, [2004] 2 AC 323 at [20] (Lord Bingham).

[52] There is a rich literature on the development of the *Ullah* doctrine; see eg P Craig, *UK, EU and Global Administrative Law: Foundations and Challenges* (CUP 2015) 273–80; R Clayton, 'Smoke and Mirrors: The Human Rights Act and the Impact of Strasbourg Case Law' [2012] PL 639; E Bjorge, 'The Courts and the ECHR: A Principled Approach to the Strasbourg Jurisprudence' [2013] CLJ 289.

[53] *Rabone and Another v Pennine Care NHS Trust* [2012] UKSC 2, [2012] 2 AC 72.

admitted to a psychiatric ward, whilst the European Court of Human Rights had pronounced itself only in cases concerning detained psychiatric patients.[54]

Speaking generally, even the countries which have the strongest attachment to domestic guarantees of fundamental rights nevertheless respect the standards of the European Convention on Human Rights as interpreted by the Strasbourg Court. The German Federal Constitutional Court at Karlsruhe thus takes into account the Strasbourg jurisprudence in its interpretation of the Basic Law, even in order to re-examine its own position in previous cases, as it did in the context of preventative detention.[55] Similarly, the Polish Constitutional Court has affirmed that it sees itself as being bound to rely on principles and methods of interpretation that lead to the conciliation of conflict between Polish law and the standards of the Convention.[56]

In addition to the role it plays in the maintenance and further realization of the quality of Convention rights, the European Court of Human Rights is confronted with a quantitative challenge, which, in a manner of speaking, is the price of its own success.

By reason both of the expansion of the number of Member States and of the ways in which the individual petition of the Court has been opened up, the number of applications to the Court has risen considerably, going from 5,200 in 1990 to 35,000 in 2002, only to reach the record high of 65,800 in 2013, and then diminishing slightly, to 56,250, in 2014. In excess of 60 per cent of the applications concern four countries: Ukraine (19.5 per cent of the pending applications), Italy (14.4 per cent, mostly in connection with questions of excessive length of court proceedings), Russia (14.3 per cent), and Turkey (13.6 per cent).

---

[54] The European Court quickly thereafter came to the same conclusion as the Supreme Court: M Andenas, 'Leading from the Front: Tort Law and Human Rights in *Rabone* and *Reynolds*' (2012) 128 LQR 323.

[55] BVerfGE 128, 326, *Preventative Detention II*.

[56] Polish Constitutional Court, Decision of 18 October 2004, P 8/04.

Having entered into force on 1 June 2010, Protocol 14 gave the Court the procedural means necessary to confront the challenges facing it.[57] A single judge may now reject a manifestly inadmissible or ill-founded application.[58] The absence of a significant disadvantage also becomes a criterion of admissibility.[59] A total of 90 per cent of the applications do not make it past this first stage. Those which do are decided in committees of three judges if the underlying question at issue is already the subject of well-established case-law of the Court;[60] or, if they are more complex, in a Chamber of seven judges.[61] Pilot judgments allow the Court to achieve a solution that extends beyond the particular case so as to cover all similar cases giving rise to the same issue.[62]

Significant results have been achieved by reason of the procedural improvements made by Protocol 14. A total of 86,063 cases were decided in 2014, which is substantially higher than the applications received that year. The number of pending cases, which had reached 161,000 towards the end of 2011, was in 2014 brought down to 69,900.

Composed, under the presidency of the Court, of seventeen judges, the Grand Chamber decides the most important cases. A case may be referred to it by one of the Chambers. After a judgment has been rendered by a Chamber, the parties may also demand, within three months, the referral of the case to the Grand Chamber; a committee of five judges, chaired by the president of the Court, decides on whether or not to allow such a referral.

The Court sits in its Plenary Assembly to elect its president, vice-president, and the chamber presidents, in order to appoint its registrar

---

[57] ETS 194—Human Rights (Protocol No 14), 13 May 2004.

[58] Art 7 of Prot 14; new Art 27 of the Convention.

[59] Art 12(b) of Prot 14; new Art of the Convention.

[60] Art 6 of Prot 14; new Art 26(1) of the Convention and Art 8 of Prot 14; new Art 28 of the Convention.

[61] Art 6 of Prot 14; new Art 26(1) of the Convention.

[62] See 'The Pilot-Judgment Procedure', Information note issued by the Registrar, ECtHR, p 1.

and in order to take decisions regarding the general administration of the Court's functions.

Intergovernmental conferences organized in 2010, at Interlaken in Switzerland; at Izmir in Turkey in 2011; at Brighton in 2012; and at Brussels in 2015, reaffirmed the attachment of the Member States to the Convention, whilst also underlining the necessity of respecting the States' margins of appreciation, what an English lawyer might call the discretion allowed to each State in interpreting and applying the European Convention on Human Rights.[63]

Thus, during a speech given in January 2012 before the Parliamentary Assembly of the Council of Europe, Prime Minister David Cameron encouraged the Court to accord to the States a broader margin of appreciation and to concentrate on the most pressing questions. The declaration adopted by the intergovernmental conference at Brighton invited the States to apply the Convention themselves and underlined the importance of subsidiarity and the margin of appreciation.[64] It made certain proposed amendments to the Convention, reducing from six to four months the time-limit within which an application may be made to the Court following the date of a final domestic decision, introducing the possibility of the highest courts and tribunals of a State Party to request the Court to render advisory opinions, and raised the retirement age to 74 years.[65] Protocols 15 and 16, which are in the process of ratification, flesh out in conventional terms these various recommendations.[66]

So far as substantive law is concerned, the Court takes into account national traditions and, as a function of how strongly held they are, will accord to the States a generous margin of appreciation at times. Thus it has held, by way of example, that neither the exclusion from

---

[63] P Mahoney, 'The Relationship between the Strasbourg Court and the National Courts' (2014) 130 LQR 568, 570.

[64] See generally P Mahoney, 'The Relationship between the Strasbourg Court and the National Courts' (2014) 130 LQR 568, 570.

[65] See eg M Elliott, 'After Brighton: Between a Rock and a Hard Place' [2012] PL 620.

[66] CETS 213—Human Rights (Protocol No 15) 24 June 2013; CETS 214—Human Rights (Protocol No 16), 2 November 2013.

the German public services of extremists[67] nor the Irish prohibition of divorce[68] was contrary to the principles of the Convention. It has allowed the dissolution of political parties in Spain connected with the terrorist organization ETA.[69] On sensitive questions relating to social relations, it has determined that the presence of crucifixes in public schools in Italy was not contrary to the demands of the right to religious freedom,[70] and that the French law of 11 October 2010 prohibiting the concealment of one's face in public places was not disproportionately restrictive given the aims it sought to achieve in terms of what the Grand Chamber termed 'living together' (another Convention term that sounds rather better in the Court's other official language than it does in English: *vivre ensemble*).[71]

The Court ensures that those rights under the Convention which are absolute—the right to life, the prohibition of torture, of slavery and of forced labour—are respected under all circumstances. Thus the fight against terrorism does not justify that a State should be allowed to expose anyone, by removing them to another country, to torture or inhuman treatment.[72]

Exercising a rigorous proportionality review of interferences which are 'necessary in a democratic society' and may be made to the non-absolute rights, the Court has adopted an extensive reading of the provisions of the Convention, such as the right to respect for family and private law, or invasions of the enjoyment of one's possessions. It has also shown itself to be particularly vigilant as regards the prohibition of any kind of discrimination in the exercise of the rights protected by the Convention.

---

[67] *Glasenapp v Germany* (1987) 9 EHRR 25.

[68] *Johnston v Ireland* (1987) 9 EHRR 203.

[69] *Batasuna v Spain* (unreported) App Nos 25803/04 and 25817/04 judgment 30 June 2009.

[70] *Lautsi v Italy* (2012) 54 EHRR 3.

[71] *SAS v France* (2015) 60 EHRR 11. See I Trispiotis, 'Two Interpretations of "Living Together" in European Human Rights Law' [2016] CLJ 580.

[72] *Chahal v United Kingdom* (1997) 23 EHRR 413; *Saadi v Italy* (2009) 49 EHRR 30; *Daoudi v France* (unreported) App No 19576/08 judgment 3 December 2009.

The Court has taken seriously the effectiveness of the rights and requirements of good administration of justice. It has accorded full effect to the right to an independent and impartial judge set out in Article 6 of the Convention and of the right to an effective remedy in Article 13.

The Court has also pointed to the central position occupied by the rights enshrined in Article 6, 'which reflects the fundamental principle of the rule of law'.[73] Relying on concepts in part fashioned by the Court itself, such as the equality of arms, the theory of appearances, or the distinction between subjective and objective impartiality, it has defined certain procedural standards by which all courts are bound. The Court's jurisprudence thus throws its weight behind the English judicial adage, expressed in 1924 by Chief Justice Lord Hewart, according to which: 'it is of fundamental importance that justice should not only be done, but should manifestly and undoubtedly be seen to be done'.[74] The requirements set out by the Court are strict in the matter of court access, the excessive length of court proceedings, the respect accorded to the rights of the defence and the presumption of innocence, as well as the execution of court judgments.

Often the jurisprudence of the Court reveals certain lacunae in domestic legislation, including in that of countries, such as the United Kingdom and France, who pioneered the protection of human rights. Thus, to name but some examples, its judgments resulted in the de-penalization of homosexuality in Northern Ireland,[75] the provision of free access to an interpreter during criminal proceedings in Germany and France, the abolition of physical punishment in British schools,[76] the recognition in France and in the United Kingdom of the rights of transsexuals to civil status,[77] and the admission of women into the German army. In relation to constitutional standards, the Court's jurisprudence developed

---

[73] *Sunday Times v United Kingdom* (1979–80) 2 EHRR 245 at [55].
[74] *R v Sussex Justices, ex p McCarthy* [1924] 1 KB 256, 259.
[75] *Dudgeon v United Kingdom* (1982) 4 EHRR 149.
[76] *Campbell and Cossans v United Kingdom* (1982) 4 EHRR 531.
[77] *Goodwin v United Kingdom* (2002) 35 EHRR 18.

the requirements flowing from Article 6,[78] which were taken into account during the wholesale reform of the French system of pretrial detention by the law of 14 April 2011; the same was the case in the matter of detained psychiatric patients.[79]

By virtue of Article 39 of the Rules of Court, it may in addition indicate interim measures,[80] which are meant to preserve the interests of the parties in the proceedings and which are binding on the States.[81] The number of such measures has risen greatly in cases concerning the forcible removal of non-nationals to their country of origin. The Court indicated interim measures before it rendered its judgment on the merits in the case of the contested treatment of Vincent Lambert.[82] The influence of the Court's jurisprudence on domestic law is all the greater due to the fact that it applies in conjunction with the law of the European Union.

3. THE LAW OF THE EUROPEAN UNION AND THE EUROPEAN CONVENTION ON HUMAN RIGHTS

In spite of the important differences between them, the law of the European Union and the law of the European Convention on Human Rights are both a part of what could be called the construct of European law.

The differences concern in the first place the particular characteristics of each legal regime. Although all the Member States of the

---

[78] *Salduz v Turkey* (2009) 49 EHRR 19; *Dayanan v Turkey* (unreported) App No 7377/03 judgment 13 October 2009.

[79] *Baudoin v France* (unreported) App No 35935/03 judgment 18 November 2010.

[80] See C Miles, 'The Influence of the International Court of Justice on the Law of Provisional Measures' in M Andenas and E Bjorge (eds), *A Farewell to Fragmentation: Reassertion and Convergence in International Law* (CUP 2015) 218, 228–30.

[81] See Juge des référés du Conseil d'État, 30 June 2009, *Ministre de l'intérieur, de l'outre-mer et des collectivités territoriales c/M.*

[82] *Lambert v France* (2016) 62 EHRR 2.

European Union are signatories to the European Convention, the ambit of the Union, much greater than that of the Convention, does not apply to as many States as does the Convention. The European Union aims to construct an integrated legal order, of general application, whereas the Convention, which is specialized in terms of its object, is more of a traditional international treaty.

Whilst both legal orders have a court of law tasked with the supervision of the principles on which they are based, there are noticeable differences between these two European courts.

Accessible only to States, to institutions, and (through preliminary references) to courts, the Court of Justice of the European Union receives only a few hundred cases per year, whereas the European Court of Human Rights, which through individual petition is open to the 800 million citizens of the forty-seven Member States of the Council of Europe, receives several tens of thousands of applications per year. The possibility, afforded to the domestic supreme courts through Protocol 16, of requesting the European Court of Human Rights to give advisory opinions on principles concerning the interpretation and application of the Convention will, however, when the Protocol enters into force, introduce bonds between the Strasbourg Court and the domestic courts inspired by those which exist between the latter and the Luxembourg Court.

Working with their référendaires,[83] the judges of the Luxembourg Court themselves personally work on every case filed to the Court, whereas the judges of the Strasbourg Court depend more and more on the instruction and the introductory research of the agents of the Court's registry in a great number of cases.

Even the methods of work differ between the two courts. The working methods of the Court of Justice are similar to those of a French court: hearing the conclusions of an Advocate General in complex cases, the absence of any indication as to the majority at which

---

[83] See foonote 12.

a decision is reached, and the lack of any dissenting opinions. The European Court of Human Rights follows a rather more Anglo-Saxon approach: both at the hearing and in the text of the document containing the Court's judgment (which will set out the majority at which it is decided as well as the opinions of individual judges), those judges who wish to do so will express their own point of view.

These important differences do not, however, prevent the law of the European Union and the European Convention on Human Rights from growing closer and closer.

The jurisprudence of the Luxembourg Court began to include fundamental rights in the general principles of community law[84] at an early stage. Then the Court, on the basis of the fact that the Member States all adhered to the European Convention,[85] incorporated the law of the Convention into community law, determining that 'in the Community legal system, the fundamental rights guaranteed by the ECHR are protected as general principles of Community law.'[86] This jurisprudence was codified by the Treaties, from the Treaty of Maastricht onwards, the latter providing in Article F(2) that:

> The Union shall respect fundamental rights, as guaranteed by the European Convention for the Protection of Human Rights and Fundamental Freedoms ... and as they result from the constitutional traditions common to the Member States, as general principles of Community law.

The Court of Justice takes care to interpret the European Convention in light of the jurisprudence of the European Court of Human Rights. On the whole it attaches increasing importance to human rights. The protection of the right to freedom of association is thus a legitimate

---

[84] Case 29–69 *Stauder* ECLI:EU:C:1969:57; Case 11–70 *Internationale Handelsgesellschaft* ECLI:EU:C:1970:114.

[85] Case 36–75 *Rutili* ECLI:EU:C:1975:137.

[86] Case C–238/99P *Limburgse Vinyl Maatschappij* ECLI:EU:C:2002:582 at [170].

reason on the basis of which the right to free movement can be restricted, so long as the restriction is proportionate.[87] A decision taken with a view to applying a Security Council Resolution concerning the assets of persons connected with terrorist networks does not relieve a Member State of the duty to respect, under the control of the Court, fundamental rights, and in this connection the European Convention on Human Rights has 'special significance'.[88]

Conversely, the European Court of Human Rights has taken the view that there is a presumption, which however is rebuttable, that secondary EU legislation respects the rights protected by the European Convention.[89] The Court has also sought to guarantee the right to a preliminary ruling from the Court of Justice, taking the view that a denial of a preliminary ruling might constitute a breach of the right of access to a court.[90]

The demands of the Convention may, however, at times create difficulties in the application of EU law. Thus, according to *MSS v Belgium*, in view of the insufficient protection accorded by Greece to asylum seekers, the removal of an asylum seeker from one European country to Greece constitutes a breach of the rights of the Convention, even though it is pronounced through application of the Dublin Regulation on the mechanisms for determining the Member State responsible for examining an application for international protection.[91] The Court of Justice has acceded to this position, taking the view that the presumption of respect for fundamental rights is rebuttable and that the situation in Greece, considered in light of *MSS v Belgium*, amounted to 'a systemic deficiency in the asylum procedure and in the reception conditions of asylum seekers'.[92]

---

[87] Case C–112/00 *Schmidberger* ECLI:EU:C:2003:333.
[88] Case C–402/05 P *Kadi and Al Barakaat International Foundation* ECLI:EU:C:2008:461 at [5].
[89] *Bosphorus Airways v Ireland* (2006) 42 EHRR 1.
[90] *Dhabi v Italy* App No 17120/09 judgment 8 April 2014.
[91] *MSS v Belgium* (2011) 53 EHRR 2.
[92] Cases C–411/10 and C–493/10 *NS and ME* ECLI:EU:C:2011:865 at [89].

Three stages of the development towards closer alignment between the two bodies of law were traversed by the Treaty of Lisbon.

First, and generally, Article 2 of the Treaty on European Union sets out clearly the values on which the Union is founded, and Article 7 establishes a mechanism of penalizing States in case of grave and persistent breaches of those values.

Secondly, the Treaty of Lisbon confers on the Charter of Fundamental Rights,[93] adopted on 7 December 2000, the same value as that of the Union Treaties. Although its ambit is broader, the Charter restates, often in identical terms, the guarantees set out by the European Convention. In this way the substantive alignment between the law of the Union and that of the Convention is reinforced.

It is all the more important that the Court of Justice has begun to review secondary Union legislation against the background of the Charter.[94] It thus invalidated entirely the Directive of 15 March 2006 on the retention of data of electronic communications services, which it held to be contrary to the demands of Article 7 on the protection of privacy and Article 8 on the protection of personal data.[95]

In relation to the States, the Court of Justice has adopted a broad conception of the effects of the Charter. According to Article 51, the Charter applies to the Member States 'only when they are implementing Union law'. The Court has held that domestic regulation concerning fiscal sanctions in connection with tax surcharges fell within the scope of European Union law, since 'the fundamental rights guaranteed by the Charter must … be complied with where national legislation falls within the scope of European Union law'.[96] By relying on the scope of EU law for the ambit of the Charter, the Court has taken an extensive approach.

---

[93] Charter of Fundamental Rights of the European Union, [2010] OJ C83/389.

[94] Case C–236/09 *Association belge des consommateurs test-achats ASBL* ECLI:EU:C:2011:100.

[95] Case C–293/12 *Digital Rights Ireland* ECLI:EU:C:2014:238.

[96] Case C–617/10 *Åklagaren v Hans Åkerberg Fransson* ECLI:EU:C:2013:105.

Finally, on an institutional level, the Treaty of Lisbon authorizes the accession of the Union to the European Convention on Human Rights. Although, according to an Opinion of the Court of Justice from 1996,[97] the European Community could not (in view of its competences) join the Convention, with the passing of time the view has been taken that the European Union should become a full member of the Convention. Reciprocally, Protocol 14 to the European Convention of Human Rights introduces to Article 59 of the Convention a provision according to which '[t]he European Union may accede to this Convention'.

However, the determination of the methods of accession has proven difficult. In its Opinion rendered on 18 December 2014,[98] the Court of Justice held that the draft agreement on accession negotiated by the Commission was not compatible with EU law. Three considerations supported this view. The draft agreement did not contain sufficient measures that would guarantee the monopoly of the Court of Justice with respect to the interpretation of EU law and especially of the Charter of Fundamental Rights; at the very least there would have to be co-ordination between the two courts in this regard. The draft agreement did not, secondly, guarantee that, with regard to questions in which the EU has competence, the relations between the States and the Union are governed only by EU law, the latter being based on mutual trust between those Member States. Finally, although matters of the common foreign and security policy fall outside the ambit of judicial review by the Court of Justice, on the basis of the accession as provided for in the draft agreement, the European Court of Human Rights would be empowered to rule on such matters, effectively entrusting to a non-EU body exclusive judicial review of EU acts, actions, or omissions in these matters. By virtue of Article 218(11) of the TFEU, the Opinion is binding and the agreement envisaged may not enter into force unless it is amended.

---

[97] C–2/94 *Opinion 2/94* ECLI:EU:C:1996:140.
[98] C–2/13 *Opinion 2/13* ECLI:EU:C:2014:2454.

Certainly the obstacles set out by the Court of Justice are not insuperable. However, they do render the effective accession of the Union to the Convention uncertain. In spite of these difficulties the two sources of human rights in Europe are however converging, combining by degrees to constitute a European legal order in which the different domestic legal systems also have a role to play.

4

European and Domestic Law

> No one can be prevented from immediately issuing their own
> European identity card, from proclaiming themselves a citizen
> of Europe or, despite the existence of borders, from fraternally
> considering our diverse world as a unified whole.
>
> —Stefan Zweig, *La Pensée européenne* (1929)

Together with the law of the European Union and the European
Convention on Human Rights, the domestic legal systems of the
countries of Europe combine to form a European legal system, whose
identity is increasingly affirming itself.

This European law is particularly evident within the field of public
law. On the one hand, the question of the co-existence of European
and domestic law in terms of hierarchy of norms, of competences of
institutions, and the role of the courts is largely a question of public
law. On the other hand, although the other branches of law—civil law,
corporate law, even criminal law—are also experiencing the influence
of European law, there can be no doubt that in those fields national
particularities remain more pronounced.

The combination, within European public law, of EU law, the law of
the European Convention, and of domestic law cannot be conceived
of along the lines of a pyramidal hierarchy of the kind developed by

Towards a European Public Law. First Edition. Bernard Stirn. © Bernard Stirn 2017.
Published 2017 by Oxford University Press.

Hans Kelsen.[1] Every element is a whole that does not have a hierarchical relationship to the other elements. But their application necessitates reasoning along the lines of 'ordered pluralism' ('*pluralisme
ordonné*'), in the instructive expression of Mireille Delmas-Marty.[2]
In a speech given on 31 January 2014, at the opening of the judicial
year in the European Court of Human Rights,[3] the President of the
German Federal Constitutional Court, Andreas Voßkuhle, evoca-
tively compared European law to Calder's mobile, of which the constituent parts find their equilibrium over and over again by constantly
depending on each other in an incessant movement. He concluded by
citing Alexander Calder: 'when everything goes right, a mobile is a
piece of poetry that dances with the joy of life and surprises.'[4]

The coming together of European law and domestic law takes place
on the basis of a common understanding, first, of the hierarchy of
norms; secondly, of the characteristics of an integrated legal order of
the European Union; and, thirdly, of certain shared guiding principles.

1. A COMMON UNDERSTANDING OF
THE HIERARCHY OF NORMS

In all of the countries of the European Union, where both the law of
the European Union and the European Convention apply, the combination of European and domestic law has amounted to a redefini-
tion of the legal system. A common understanding has progressively
emerged, and it has two bases: first, the superiority of European law
over domestic statutory law is fully recognized; and, secondly, the co-
existence of European law and domestic constitutional rules implies

---

[1] See eg H Kelsen, *Introduction to the Problems of Legal Theory* (BL Paulson and SL
Paulson trs, Clarendon Press 2002 [1934]).
[2] M Delmas-Marty, *Ordering Pluralism: A Conceptual Framework for Understanding
the Transnational Legal World* (N Norberg tr, Hart Publishing 2009).
[3] A Voßkuhle, 'Pyramid or Mobile? Human Rights Protection by the European
Constitutional Courts' in *Dialogue between Judges* (Council of Europe 2014) 36.
[4] ibid 40.

conciliatory interpretations, which allow for normative harmony without sounding in superiority.

European Law and Domestic Statutory Law

Monism and Dualism

Certain European States—especially Italy and the United Kingdom—have kept a dualist conception of the relationship between international and domestic law, according to which the passing of a statute is necessary for a treaty to have domestic legal effect.

Thus EU law applies in the United Kingdom by virtue of the European Communities Act 1972, to which was added the European Union Act 2011, which underscores the importance of a domestic statute of incorporation. Similarly, although the United Kingdom was the first country to ratify it, on 8 March 1951, the European Convention on Human Rights did not in strict terms have any effect in domestic law until the adoption, in 1998, of the Human Rights Act, which came on stream on 2 October 2000.

Following a similar path, the Italian Constitution of 27 December 1947 makes the introduction of an international treaty into the domestic legal order dependent on incorporating legislation. The European Convention on Human Rights was made directly applicable in Italy through the law of 4 August 1955. A constitutional revision of 18 October 2001, entering into force in 2006, did admittedly create an obligation for statute law to respect international obligations. But this constitutional requirement did not do away with the need, after the ratification of a treaty, for legislation which incorporates into domestic law the treaty at issue. Within that framework, the Corte costituzionale characterized the European Convention on Human Rights as an intermediary norm—'*una norma interposta*'—between the constitution and international law: a statute may be disapplied by reason of breach of the Convention; but only by the Constitutional Court, to which the other courts must defer the question, as the subject is one concerning rights protected by the constitutional order.[5] This jurisprudence has, however, been contested by the Consiglio di Stato which, treating the European Convention and EU law similarly, takes the view that the ordinary courts are competent to set aside the application of a statute which is in breach of the Convention.[6]

More numerous are those countries which—in common with France from the constitutional regimes of 1946 and onwards—have opted for a monist conception, according to which, from the point of ratification and publication, an international treaty is a part of domestic law, becoming the law of the land. The legislator is, however, not entirely shut out of the process: according to Article 53 of the Constitution of 1958, the most important treaties, and especially those concerning matters of a legislative nature, may be ratified or approved only after legislative authorization has been secured.

Such a moderated monism can also be found in Germany, where international treaties are applicable within domestic law but only after approbation has been given in legislation.

Self-executing Treaties

The consequences of the distinction between monism and dualism is tempered by the concept, common to all domestic legal systems, of direct effect.[7] The application of a treaty within domestic law presumes, for its provisions to produce any effect, that they create rights on which individuals may usefully rely; if that is not the case, the treaty will not be self-executing and it will lack direct effect. The Conseil d'État, in its judgment in the 2012 case *GISTI*, taking a position inspired by views commonly held elsewhere, decided that it would give direct effect to a provision of a treaty:

---

[5] Corte costituzionale, Decisions of 24 and 31 October 2007.

[6] Consiglio di Stato, Decision of 2 March 2010.

[7] See eg *Hoogenraad v Organization for Research in the Netherlands* (1990) 96 ILR 389, 390–1; *Resolution No 5 of 10 October (Resolution adopted by the Plenum of the Supreme Court of the Russia Federation)* (2003) 150 ILR 726, 729–30; *Boyce and Another v the Queen (Barbados)* [2004] UKPC 32, (2004) 134 ILR 439, 446.

when, taking into account the intention of the parties and the general economy of the treaty at issue, as well as the contents and terms, the provision does not aim only to govern relations between States and does not necessitate the intervention of any additional act in order to have effects vis-à-vis individuals.[8]

The European Court of Justice, which is the only body competent to decide on the direct effect of the treaties concluded by the European Union as well as the EU Treaties, takes the same approach, by virtue of a division of competence between the Union and the Member States.[9] Thus a treaty which, as is the case with the European Convention on Human Rights, aims to guarantee fundamental rights is, in accordance with these criteria, self-executing in all its provisions.

Superiority of Treaties over Statute

However international law is received into domestic law, the constitutional and supreme courts of Europe have recognized the primacy of international law over domestic statutory law, in a move initiated by the Belgian Cour de cassation in a decision of 27 May 1971,[10] followed in short order by the German Federal Constitutional Court, in a ruling of 9 June 1971.[11] The same position was taken by the Italian Constitutional Court in respect of Community law, on 30 October 1975,[12] and then, in a ruling handed down on 8 June 1984, in respect of international law in its entirety.[13]

In France, the superiority of treaties over statute was affirmed by Article 55 of the constitution, which provides that 'Treaties or

---

[8] Conseil d'État, Plenary Assembly, 11 April 2012, *GISTI*.

[9] Case C–240/09 *Lesoochranárske zoskupenie VLK* ECLI:EU:C:2011:125.

[10] *Minister for Economic Affairs v SA Fromagerie Franco–Suisse 'Le Ski'* (1971) 93 ILR 203.

[11] *Alfons Lütticke GMBH ('Milk Powder')* (1971) 93 ILR 358.

[12] *ICIC v Ministero Commercio Estero* (1975) 93 ILR 526, (1977) 3 Italian Yearbook of International Law 369.

[13] *Granital SpA v Amministrazione delle Finanze dello Stato* (1984) 93 ILR 527.

agreements duly ratified or approved shall, upon publication, prevail over Acts of Parliament, subject, with respect to each agreement or treaty, to its application by the other party.'

The French Conseil constitutionnel has held that the question of the conformity of a statute with treaties does not fall within the ambit of constitutional review exercised by the constitutional judges before a statute is passed.[14] It set out the division of labour in the application by French authorities of Article 55, pointing out that 'it is incumbent on the various organs of the State to ensure the application of international treaties within the framework of their respective competences'.[15]

The Conseil constitutionnel reaffirmed its jurisprudence after the introduction of so-called priority preliminary rulings on constitutionality ('*question prioritaire de constitutionnalité*', QPC), which gives the right to any person involved in legal proceedings before a French court to argue that a statutory provision infringes constitutionally guaranteed rights and freedoms. Its judgment of 12 May 2010, *Online Betting and Gambling*, was particularly explicit, distinguishing expressly 'between the review of statutes for the purpose of verifying their conformity with the Constitution, which is incumbent upon the Constitutional Council, and the review of their compatibility with the international and European commitments of France, which is incumbent upon the courts of law and administrative courts'.[16]

Against this background the Cour de cassation decided, in its judgment of 24 May 1975, *Société Cafés Jacques Vabre*, that it was incumbent on the ordinary law courts to refrain from applying statutes, even more recent ones, which are incompatible with the provisions of an international treaty.[17] As for the French administrative courts,

---

[14] *Re Law on the Voluntary Termination of Pregnancy* (1975) 74 ILR 523.
[15] Decision of 3 September 1986, No 86–216.
[16] Decision of 12 May 2010, No 2010–605 at [11].
[17] *Administration des Douanes v Société Cafés Jacques Vabre et Weigel* (1975) 93 ILR 240.

which sit in cases concerning the obligations of the Executive, there was greater difficulty in freeing oneself from the constitutional task of applying statutory law in case of incompatibility of a statute and a rule of international law.

A treaty which was subsequent to a statute and incompatible with it would in French law plainly be taken to have abrogated the statute. More difficult was the question of the relationship between a treaty and a subsequent statute. Having for a period applied the theory according to which the statute operated as a screen behind which the court was not authorized to look ('*la loi écran*'),[18] the Conseil d'État then, through its judgment in *Nicolo* of 20 October 1989,[19] fell into line with the domestic and European courts by holding that the application of a statute, even one more recent than the treaty, must be set aside by the administrative court if it is incompatible with France's international obligations.[20]

Review of Compatibility with International Treaties

In France the ordinary courts and the administrative courts both safeguard the superiority of international treaties over statutes, referred to in French law as review of conventionality ('*contrôle de conventionnalité*'), and this has profoundly reshaped their judicial review of legislation. This kind of review is also exercised by the Conseil constitutionnel whenever it sits not as a constitutional court but in its capacity as an electoral court.[21] The same goes for the Tribunal des Conflits, the final arbiter in deciding questions of conflicts of jurisdiction between the ordinary and the administrative courts,[22] in cases

---

[18] Conseil d'État, decision of 1 March 1968, *Syndicat Général de Fabricants de Semoules de France*; Conseil d'État, 13 May 1983, *Société Anonyme René Moline*.

[19] *Re Nicolo and Another* (1989) 93 ILR 286.

[20] See LN Brown and JS Bell, *French Administrative Law* (5th edn, OUP 1998) 284–5.

[21] *Re Election for the Fifth Constituency of Val d'Oise* (1988) 111 ILR 496.

[22] See LN Brown and JS Bell, *French Administrative Law* (5th edn, OUP 1998) 149–56.

where the determination of which court is competent depends on the application of a statute of which the conventionality is disputed.[23]

Notwithstanding the fact that it is the home of parliamentary sovereignty, where nothing seems to be equal to frustrating the will of parliament,[24] the United Kingdom, too, has gone down the route of judicial review of the compatibility of statutes with international treaties. Thus, having had the benefit of a preliminary reference to the Court of Justice, the Appellate Committee of the House of Lords in *Factortame* held, on the basis of the European Communities Act 1972, that when Community law conflicts with a statute the courts will disapply the latter.[25] Even by 1977 Lord Denning emphasized the importance of the jurisprudence of the Court of Justice in relation to the application of Community law: 'Just as in Rome, you should do as Rome does. So in the European Community, you should do as the European Court does.'[26] Beyond EU law, the House of Lords, in the case of the extradition to Chile of General Pinochet,[27] which did not concern statutory law, gave precedence over domestic law to the UN Torture Convention[28] on the question of the determination of the scope of waiver of immunity of state officials.[29] In the landmark *Belmarsh* case, handed down on 16 December 2004,[30] the House of Lords held that certain provisions of the Anti-Terrorism, Crime, and Security Act 2001 were incompatible with the European Convention on Human Rights.[31] In his judgment in the case, Lord

---

[23] Tribunal des Conflits, 13 December 2010, *Société Green Yellow et autres c/ EDF*.

[24] Cf *Moohan v The Lord Advocate* [2014] UKSC 67, [2014] WLR 544 at [29] (Lord Hodge).

[25] *R v Secretary of State for Transport, Ex p Factortame Ltd (No 2)* [1991] 1 AC 603.

[26] Lord Denning, *The Discipline of Law* (Butterworths 1979) 20–1.

[27] *R v Bow Street Metropolitan Stipendiary Magistrate, Ex parte Pinochet Ugarte (No 3)* [2000] 1 AC 147, (1999) 119 ILR 135.

[28] Convention against Torture and Other Cruel, Inhuman or Degrading Treatment or Punishment, 10 December 1984, 1465 UNTS 85.

[29] See C McLachlan, *Foreign Relations Law* (CUP 2014) 109–10.

[30] *A v Secretary of State for the Home Department ('Belmarsh')* [2004] UKHL 56, [2005] 2 AC 68.

[31] See R Clayton, 'The Belmarsh Case' in S Juss and M Sunkin (eds), *Landmark Judgments in Public Law* (Hart Publishing 2017) Ch 7.

Hoffmann observed: 'This is one of the most important cases which the House has had to decide in recent years. It calls into question the very existence of an ancient liberty of which this country has until now been very proud: freedom from arbitrary arrest and detention.'[32]

This jurisprudence has since been upheld and applied by the Supreme Court of the United Kingdom in cases concerning domestic statutory law and European law.[33]

European Law and Domestic Constitutional Law

Europe and Constitutions

Although the treaty establishing a constitution for Europe[34] was abandoned following the negative referenda in the spring of 2005 in the Netherlands and France, the European order nevertheless has a constitutional dimension. Thus, the Court of Justice has characterized the Treaty establishing the European Economic Community as a 'basic constitutional charter',[35] adding that 'albeit concluded in the form of an international agreement', it 'none the less constitutes the constitutional charter of a Community based on the rule of law', in which 'the States have limited their sovereign rights, in ever wider fields, and the subjects of which comprise not only Member States but also their nationals'.[36] For its part the European Court of Human Rights has characterized the European Convention as a 'constitutional instrument of European public order ("*ordre public*")'.[37]

---

[32] *A v Secretary of State for the Home Department ('Belmarsh')* [2004] UKHL 56, [2005] 2 AC 68 at [86].

[33] See B Dickson, *Human Rights in the UK Supreme Court* (OUP 2013).

[34] Treaty Establishing a Constitution for Europe, 29 October 2004, [2004] OJ C310/1 (never entered into force).

[35] Case 294/83 *Parti écologiste 'Les Verts' v European Parliament* ECLI:EU:C:1986:166 at [23].

[36] Opinion 1/91 on the European Economic Area ECLI:EU:C:1991:490 at [21].

[37] *Loizidou v Turkey (Preliminary Objections)* (1995) 20 EHRR 99, (1995) 103 ILR 622, 646.

These declarations must be reconciled with municipal legal orders in which the constitution is supreme, although the latter increasingly has given European law special status. Most of the constitutions of the Member States of the Union mention the European Union explicitly. Some constitutions also make reference to the European Convention on Human Rights, giving it too a special status.

The French Constitution did not contain any particular provision pertaining to European law until the revision of 25 June 1992, a condition to the ratification of the Treaty of Maastricht.[38] With this revision Europe entered into the Constitution, which gives it a special status, the provisions of which were modified by the constitutional revisions of 25 January 1999 and 4 February 2008, necessitated by the Treaties of Amsterdam and Lisbon. Since the entry into force of the latter, seven Articles 88-1–88-7, make up Title XV of the Constitution, entitled *On the European Union*. According to Article 88-1, which introduces the section:

> [t]he Republic shall participate in the European Union constituted by States which have freely chosen to exercise some of their powers in common by virtue of the Treaty on European Union and of the Treaty on the Functioning of the European Union, as they result from the treaty signed in Lisbon on 13 December 2007.

On the basis of these general provisions the Conseil constitutionnel has inferred that the transposition into domestic law of a community directive is a constitutional requirement;[39] from this it has drawn two consequences, both of which show the special status accorded in French law to the law of the European Union.

---

[38] See p 20 and *Re Treaty on European Union, 1992 ('Maastricht I')* (1992) 93 ILR 337.

[39] Conseil constitutionnel, Decision 2004–496 of 10 June 2004; Decision 2004–497 of 1 July 2004; Decision 2006–540 of 27 July 2006.

In the first place the Conseil constitutionnel will satisfy itself that a statute transposing a directive does not contain any provisions which are 'manifestly incompatible with the directive it is designed to transpose'.[40] Although, generally, the Conseil constitutionnel does not review legislation with a view to ascertaining whether it complies with international treaties—this being the reserve of the ordinary and administrative courts—a review of that kind, in the attenuated form of 'manifest incompatibility', is thus exercised by the Conseil constitutionnel, by reason of the constitutional requirement of transposition of directives, in relation to the statutes designed to ensure the transposition of the directive in question.

In the second place the constitutional character of this requirement of transposition has led the Conseil constitutionnel to take the view that it is not its role to pronounce on the conformity with the Constitution of a statute which does no more than 'to draw the necessary conclusions from unconditional and precise provisions' of a directive.[41] It has held that only the Court of Justice is competent to determine whether a directive conforms with the fundamental rights guarantees of the EU Treaties. A directive thus acts as a shield for the review of the domestic constitutional court, with one reservation, however, according to which 'the transposition of a Directive must not run counter to a rule or a principle inherent in the constitutional identity of France'.[42] In relation to a transposing statute the competence of the Conseil constitutionnel will not fall to be exercised except where an attack is mounted against this identity, the contours of which are still unclear.

Underlining the importance of the constitutional requirement of transposing directives in French law, the Conseil constitutionnel, by way of judicial development, gave delayed effect to a censure of legislative provisions, where an immediate declaration of

---

[40] Decision 2006–540 of 27 July 2006 at [20].   [41] ibid at [35].
[42] ibid at [19]; Decision 2008–564 19 June 2008 at [44].

unconstitutionality would have compromised the constitutional requirement. By deferring by some months the date of the effect of the unconstitutionality it declared, the Conseil constitutionnel accorded the legislator a delay period allowing the latter to replace with new transposing provisions those which were found to be contrary to the Constitution.[43]

This particular regime concerning directives, as derived from Article 88-1 of the Constitution, has the effect that, in relation to transposing legislation, the Conseil constitutionnel on the one hand exercises a measure of review based on conventionality (ie review of compliance with international treaties): but, on the other, it will be slow to find that the legislation is in breach of the Constitution.

In similar cases concerning applications directed against secondary legislation which transpose a directive, the Conseil d'État has, in setting out its course, based itself on the same principles.[44] Having acceded to the existence of a constitutional requirement of transposition of directives, the Conseil d'État in *Arcelor* held that, in order to pronounce on claims alleging that a decree assuring the transposition of an unconditional and precise directive was in breach of a constitutional principle, the administrative court must first ascertain whether EU law guarantees effective protection of that principle. If that is the case, then all the claims which do not give rise to serious difficulty will be rejected as unfounded; if such a difficulty does in fact arise, a preliminary reference must be made to the Court of Justice, as 'only the Court of Justice is competent to declare invalid acts of the Community institutions'.[45] Only in the absence of effective protection by EU law of the constitutional principle invoked may a domestic court review the conformity of the impugned decree with that principle.

---

[43] Decision 2008–564 19 June 2008.
[44] Conseil d'État, 8 February 2007, *Société Arcelor Atlantique et Lorraine*.
[45] Case 314/85 *Foto Frost* ECLI:EU:C:1987:452 at [11].

Similar reasoning was adopted by the Conseil d'État when the conformity with the European Convention on Human Rights of a Directive was challenged before it.[46] The reason such a claim could lie in the first place is, as we have seen,[47] that the Court of Justice had held that, in the EU legal order, the fundamental rights guaranteed by the Convention are protected as general principles of Community law.[48] In case of serious difficulty, the domestic court must make a preliminary reference to the Court of Justice, as only it is competent to declare invalid acts of the Community institutions. As constitutional norms are not at issue there is no limit here to the obligation of reference.

These lines of cases show the delicate character of the interaction of constitutional principles and the law of the European Union.

The Constitution and the Law of the European Union: the Logistics of Conciliation

The supremacy of the Constitution and the primacy of the legal order of the European Union may seem to contradict one another. But the domestic constitutional principles are scarcely different, in terms of their content, from those on which the European legal order rests. For that reason the necessary conciliation of the two superiorities is possible.

The primacy of the Community legal order was established very early by the Court of Justice.[49] That is one of the foundations of the legal order of the European Union which must necessarily be respected by the Member States; they cannot invoke provisions of their national constitutions in order to free themselves of this obligation.[50] This might seem to be in opposition to the supremacy of the Constitution which, in respect of French municipal law, has been set

---

[46] Conseil d'État, 10 April 2008, *Conseil national des barreaux*.
[47] See p 75 of this volume.
[48] Case C-238/99P *Limburgse Vinyl Maatschappij* ECLI:EU:C:2002:582.
[49] Case 6-64 *Costa v ENEL* ECLI:EU:C:1964:66; Case 106/77 *Simmenthal* ECLI:EU:C:1978:49.
[50] Case C-399/11 *Melloni* ECLI:EU:C:2013:107.

out in similar terms by all the highest courts: the Conseil d'État,[51] the Cour de cassation,[52] and the Conseil constitutionnel.[53]

So far as Italy is concerned, the Italian Constitutional Court ensures the compliance of the principles of the Italian constitutional order;[54] this involves requirements of European law as well as of general international law. At the suit of Germany, the International Court of Justice held in *Jurisdictional Immunities of the State (Germany v Italy)* that Italy had breached the jurisdictional immunities which under international law accrued to Germany, by reason of the Corte di cassazione having determined that Italian courts had jurisdiction over claims bearing on violations of international humanitarian law committed by the German Reich in 1943–45.[55] The International Court's judgment did not stop the Italian Constitutional Court from holding the statute adopted in order to bring Italian law into compliance with the judgment to be in breach of the fundamental rights guaranteed by the Constitution.[56]

The Spanish Constitutional Court, too, is dedicated to the supremacy of the Constitution within the municipal legal order;[57] as is the Polish Constitutional Court, the latter having proclaimed that 'the Constitution is the supreme source of law of the Polish Republic.'[58]

Since its judgments in *Solange I*, from 29 May 1974;[59] *Solange II*, from 22 October 1986;[60] and *Solange III*, from 7 June 2000,[61] the

---

[51] Conseil d'État, 30 Octobrer 1998, *Sarran and Levacher*.
[52] Cour de cassation, 2 June 2000, *Pauline Fraisse*.
[53] Decision No 2004–505 of 19 November 2004.
[54] *Fragd v Amministrazione delle Finance dello Stato* (1989) 93 ILR 538.
[55] *Jurisdictional Immunities of the State (Germany v Italy)*, ICJ Rep 2012, p 99.
[56] *Simoncioni, Alessi, and Bergamini v Federal Republic of Germany and Presidency of the Council of Ministers* (2014) 24 Italian Yearbook of International Law 488.
[57] Spanish Constitutional Court, Decisions of 13 December 2004 and 9 June 2005.
[58] Polish Constitutional Court, Decisions of 19 December 2006 and 16 November 2011.
[59] *Internationale Handelsgesellschaft ('Solange I')* (1974) 93 ILR 362.
[60] *Wünsche Handelsgesellschaft ('Solange II')* (1986) 93 ILR.
[61] *Bananenmarktordnung ('Solange III')* BVerfGE 102, 147.

German Federal Constitutional Court has shown itself willing to protect particularly jealously the fundamental rights guaranteed by the German Basic Law of 1949. Community law takes precedence only so long as it respects these rights. In its judgment of 30 June 2009 the Court, whilst determining that Germany could ratify the Lisbon Treaty, strongly emphasized the requirements of democracy and protection of fundamental rights flowing from the Basic Law.[62] Similarly, it held that the creation of the European Financial Stability Facility conformed to the requirements of the Basic Law, pointing out, however, that the national parliament must retain 'control over the fundamental decisions of fiscal policy'.[63]

Although it has no single codified constitution, the legal order of the United Kingdom rests on principles of a constitutional nature. 'The United Kingdom has no written constitution, but we have a number of constitutional instruments', Lord Neuberger and Lord Mance observed in their judgment in *HS2*.[64] They include great texts such as Magna Carta 1215, the Habeas Corpus Act 1679, the Bill of Rights 1689, in addition to constitutional statutes such as the Human Rights Act 1998 and the Constitutional Reform Act 2005. In common with other European constitutional and supreme courts, the UK Supreme Court guarantees, within the domestic legal order, the supremacy of these constitutional norms. Especially instructive in this connection in the judgment of Lord Reed in *HS2*, where he observed that:

> If there is a conflict between a constitutional principle ... and EU law, that conflict has to be resolved by our courts as an issue arising under the constitutional law of the United Kingdom.[65]

---

[62] *Lisbon Treaty Constitutionality Case* (2009) 141 ILR 554.

[63] BVerfGE 132, 195 at [124].

[64] *R (on the application of HS2 Action Alliance Ltd) v Secretary of State for Transport* [2014] UKSC 3, [2014] 1 WLR 324 at [207].

[65] ibid at [79].

Whilst tensions in sovereignty may arise, the fundamental rights protected by the domestic constitutions and by the EU treaties largely overlap.

Indeed the equivalence between the two is so great that the Court of Justice extracts the general principles of European Union law from 'constitutional traditions common to the Member States'.[66] Even before the European Union was bound by the European Convention on Human Rights, the Court would take the view that the fundamental rights guaranteed by the Convention are protected as general principles of European Union law. The Charter of Fundamental Rights of the European Union reinforces this shared base of common principles.

Thus the co-existence of constitutional requirements and the principles of EU law do not give rise to more difficulty than an attentive dialogue of judges can overcome.

Tensions and blockages do, however, arise from time to time. By a decision handed down on 31 January 2012,[67] the Czech Constitutional Court for example refused to follow a decision of the Court of Justice relating to the modes of calculation of pensions of persons resident in the Czech Republic in relation to periods of work done in Slovakia before the dissolution of Czechoslovakia. In particularly virulent terms, the Czech Court observed that a:

> [f]ailure to distinguish the legal relationships arising from the dissolution of a state with a uniform social security system from the legal relationships arising for social security from the free movement of persons in the European Communities, or the European Union, is a failure to respect European history; it is comparing things that are not comparable.[68]

But such irritations, explicable by the particularities of the history of each State, remain exceptional and, for the most part, respectful understanding ends up winning the day.

---

[66] Case 11–70 *Internationale Handelsgesellschaft* ECLI:EU:C:1970:114 at [4].
[67] Pl. Us 5/12.   [68] ibid.

There is real dialogue between the domestic supreme courts. In order to hand down its *Arcelor* judgment,[69] the French Conseil d'État was particular attentive to the *Solange* jurisprudence of the German Federal Constitutional Court.[70] It arrived at a similar solution: the domestic courts rely on the Court of Justice where—the Federal Constitutional Court says 'so long as'—the fundamental rights at issue are protected by the Union.

For its part, the Court of Justice is at pains to respect the authority of domestic constitutional principles. Thus it has held that the principle of the dignity of the human person, protected both by the German Basic Law and the general principles of EU law, allowed for Germany to prohibit laser games which simulate the killing of human beings, without breaching the requirements of free movement of services.[71] Similarly the Court has held that EU law was not an obstacle to the United Kingdom extending to residents of Gibraltar voting rights in European Parliament elections.[72]

These decisions show how far the Court of Justice goes in taking into consideration domestic requirements of a constitutional nature. There are, however, limits to how far the Court is willing to go in stretching a point. So the abrupt lowering, from 70 to 62, of the compulsory retirement age of judges in Hungary was held to be disproportionate in relation to the legitimate aim invoked.[73]

Priority Preliminary Rulings on Constitutionality and the Law of the European Union

A similar effort of conciliation is evident, in France, when the requirements of EU law come up against the priority preliminary rulings on constitutionality exercised by the Conseil constitutionnel. According

---

[69] Conseil d'État, 8 February 2007, *Société Arcelor Atlantique et Lorraine*.

[70] *Internationale Handelsgesellschaft* ('Solange I') (1974) 93 ILR 362; *Wünsche Handelsgesellschaft* ('Solange II') (1986) 93 ILR; *Bananenmarktordnung* ('Solange III') BVerfGE 102.

[71] Case C–36/02 *Omega Spielhallen* ECLI:EU:C:2004:614.

[72] Case C–145/04 *Spain v United Kingdom* ECLI:EU:C:2006:543.

[73] Case C–286/12 *Commission v Hungary* ECLI:EU:C:2012:687.

to the principles set out by the Court of Justice in *Simmenthal*,[74] and consistently applied since, all domestic courts must be able to apply the law of the European Union immediately, there being no domestic law mechanism to slow down domestic judicial intervention in this connection.

This rule led the Cour de cassation, in *Abdeli and Melki*,[75] to make a preliminary reference on the compatibility with the requirements of EU law of the French priority preliminary ruling mechanism, as set out by a statute (*loi organique*) of 10 December 2009. The *Abdeli and Melki* case gave the Conseil constitutionnel occasion to set out in detail, in its decision *Online Betting and Gambling*,[76] the ways in which the review under the schema of priority preliminary rulings on constitutionality co-exist with the requirements of the law of the European Union. Although the domestic court must decide as a matter of urgency or within a given deadline, it may nevertheless apply EU law and hand down its decision without having to wait for the judgment regarding the question of constitutionality. The Conseil d'État, two days later, followed a similar course. It held in *Rujovic* that it was incumbent on the administrative courts, 'being generally competent to decide in matters relating to the application of the law of the European Union',[77] to secure the effectiveness of EU law. This includes the power to take, at any point during the process of a priority preliminary ruling on constitutionality, the necessary measures to bring to an end, in case of urgency, any possible contrary effects of domestic legislation on EU law, and if necessary to make a preliminary reference to the Court of Justice.[78]

---

[74] Case C–106/77 *Amministrazione delle Finanze dello Stato v Simmenthal SpA* ECLI:EU:C:1978:49.

[75] Cour de cassation, 16 April 2010, *Abdeli and Melki*.

[76] Decision of 12 May 2010, No 2010–605.

[77] Conseil d'État, 30 October 2009, *Mme Perreux* ('juge de droit commun de l'application du droit de l'Union européenne').

[78] Conseil d'État, 14 May 2010, *Rujovic*.

By its ruling of 22 June 2010, decided by way of accelerated procedure, the Court of Justice decided that, if the interpretation made by
the Conseil constitutionnel and the Conseil d'État was relied on, the
organic law of 10 December 2009 was not in breach of the requirements of EU law.[79] The question which the statute gave rise to in
relation to EU law was thus swiftly resolved, in a spirit of dialogic
convergence.

The process of priority preliminary rulings on constitutionality
has furthermore given the Conseil constitutionnel occasion to make
its first reference to the Court of Justice. In a case concerning a priority preliminary ruling on the constitutionality of a statute which gave
to the so-called investigation chamber of lower courts (*'la chambre
de l'instruction'*) the responsibility of effectuating the mandate of the
European Arrest Warrant, without any right of appeal for the person
concerned, the Conseil constitutionnel asked the Court of Justice
whether this non-availability of appeal was necessitated by the law of
the European Union.[80] The Court of Justice, dealing with the request
under the so-called urgent procedure, said 'no';[81] this in turn led the
Conseil constitutionnel to hold that the statutory provision at issue
was unconstitutional, as it was in breach of the constitutional right to
an effective judicial remedy.[82]

Such examples of necessary co-existence as between domestic constitutional principle and the law of the European Union do not sit
well with the conception of a pyramidal hierarchy of norms, such as
the model developed by Kelsen.[83] Two legal orders co-exist: on the
one hand, the domestic legal order, of which the Constitution is the
supreme norm and, on the other, the legal order of the European
Union, which has its own requirements. Whilst the two largely

---

[79] C–188/10 and C–189/10 *Abdeli and Melki* ECLI.EU:C:2010·363.
[80] Decision No 2013–314 of 4 April 2013.
[81] Case C–168/13 PPU *Jérémy F.* ECLI:EU:C:2013:358.
[82] Decision No 2013–314 of 14 June 2013.
[83] H Kelsen, *Introduction to the Problems of Legal Theory* (BL Paulson and SL
Paulson trs, Clarendon Press 2002 [1934]).

reinforce one another, that mutual reinforcement is only partial. The law of the European Union constitutes 'a legal order of incomplete superposition, which binds the domestic legal orders without, however, converging entirely with them', writes Professor Marie Gautier-Melleray.[84] A complex web joins together, on the one side, all of the domestic legal systems of the Member States and, on the other side, the law of the European Union. Becoming increasingly distinguishable from general international law, more and more similar to domestic law, without however taking on such characteristics entirely, the law of the European Union is characterized by particularities which are becoming increasingly clear.

2. THE INTEGRATED LEGAL ORDER OF THE EUROPEAN UNION

Being distinct both from domestic law and general international law, the law of the European Union has fashioned for itself a special kind of identity, sitting on the cusp of international law and domestic law. This special identity, safeguarded by the Court of Justice, has been strongly emphasized by the domestic courts, not least in France.

The Court of Justice, Guarantor of the Legal Order of the Union

Guardian of the unity and the authority of EU law, the Court of Justice has developed a jurisprudence that gives the European Union all due authority. From its 1963 ruling in *Van Gend en Loos* onwards, the Court has affirmed the direct effect of EU law, holding that the

---

[84] 'Le Tribunal des conflits et le "cas particulier" du droit de l'Union européenne' in *Mélanges en l'honneur du Professeur Joël Molinier* (LGDJ 2012).

Community 'constitutes a new legal order of international law for the benefit of which the States have limited their sovereign rights, albeit within limited fields, and the subjects of which comprise not only Member States but also their nationals'.[85] It then developed the principle of supremacy in *Costa v ENEL*, where it observed that, 'by contrast with ordinary international treaties, the EEC Treaty has created its own legal system'.[86] From this flows the obligation for every domestic court, in a case within its jurisdiction, to 'apply Community law in its entirety and protect rights which the latter confers on individuals and must accordingly set aside any provision of national law which may conflict with it, whether prior or subsequent to the Community rule'.[87] The Member States must co-operate loyally in order to make sure that Community law is respected within their territory.[88] A breach of this duty will mean that the State incurs liability in damages,[89] even if the breach flows from statute,[90] or from a judicial decision rendered by a domestic supreme court.[91]

These landmark rulings, rendering effective the authority of the European Union, have been followed by judgments that exhibit a certain flexibility in the application of EU law.

Thus the right to be heard does not imply that a non-national must receive the possibility to put forward their view before they are removed, if the non-national has been able to put forward their view during the hearing regarding the refusal of leave to remain.[92] Similarly, a non-national who is a European citizen may be excluded from social benefit schemes if they do not have legal residence.[93]

---

[85] Case 26–62 *Van Gend en Loos* ECLI:EU:C:1963:1.
[86] Case 6–64 *Costa v ENEL* ECLI:EU:C:1964:66.
[87] Case 106/77 *Simmenthal* ECLI:EU:C:1978:49 at [21].
[88] Case C–265/95 *Commission v France* ECLI:EU:C:1997:595.
[89] Cases C–6/90 and C–9/90 *Francovich & Bonifaci* ECLI:EU:C:1991:428.
[90] Cases C–46/93 and C–48/93 *Brasserie du Pêcheur & Factortame* ECLI:EU:C:1996:79.
[91] Case C–224/01 *Köbler* ECLI:EU:C:2003:513.
[92] Case C–249/13 *Boudjlida* ECLI:EU:C:2014:2431.
[93] Case C–333/13 *Dano* ECLI:EU:C:2014:2358.

The Legal Order of the European Union and French Courts

In its decision of 9 April 1992 regarding the Maastricht Treaty,[94] the Conseil constitutionnel observed that the European Parliament 'belongs to an independent legal order which, although integrated into the legal systems of the different Member States of the Communities, does not form part of the institutional order of the French Republic.'[95] On the basis of Article 88-1 of the Constitution, the Conseil constitutionnel in its decision of 9 August 2012 on the Treaty on Stability, Coordination and Governance in the Economic and Monetary Union held, more forthrightly, that 'the constituent authority ... enshrined the existence of a European Union legal system incorporated into the national legal order which is distinct from international law.'[96]

More and more, the jurisprudence of the Conseil d'État, too, distinguishes between the law of the European Union and other international law.

The first particularity was brought out in connection with the practice of the Prime Minister, relying on powers conferred on him by the second paragraph of Article 37 of the French Constitution, of amending through decree matters not coming under the scope of statute law.[97] The Conseil d'État held that 'given the requirements inherent to the hierarchy of norms and the obligation incumbent on domestic authorities to apply EU law', the Prime Minister must, in situations where the statutory provisions at issue were in breach of EU law, within a reasonable period and under the supervision of the courts, rely on the powers vested in him by the Constitution in order to bring domestic law in compliance with the European requirements.

---

[94] *Re Treaty on European Union, 1992 ('Maastricht I')* (1992) 93 ILR 337.

[95] ibid at [34].   [96] Decision No 2012–653 of 9 August 2012 at [8].

[97] Art 37 of the French Constitution provides: 'Matters other than those coming under the scope of statute law shall be matters for regulation. Provisions of statutory origin enacted in such matters may be amended by decree issued after consultation with the Conseil d'État. Any such provisions passed after the coming into force of the Constitution shall be amended by decree only if the Constitutional Council has found that they are matters for regulation as defined in the foregoing paragraph.'

Another French series of cases which applies only to EU law, and not to other international law, concerns state responsibility by reason of court decisions. That type of liability is, although it exists in principle, normally excluded in domestic law when what is at issue is a final judgment, such as the ruling of a supreme court.[98] The situation is different, however, in respect of EU law. In keeping with the *Köbler* jurisprudence of the Court of Justice, the Conseil d'État has taken the view that state responsibility would be engaged where a judicial decision, even a definitive one, would result in a manifest breach of European Union law.[99]

In cases concerning so-called '*référés*', that is, certain urgent cases decided by a single member bench, the judge does not, in view of his role and in particular of the brief period in which he has to reach his conclusion, in principle have powers of review of the compliance of statutes with the European Convention on Human Rights.[100] Here, too, a different solution has been reached in respect of the law of the European Union; the judge sitting in '*référés*' may set aside the application of a statute which manifestly breaches EU law.[101] Furthermore, the judge sitting in so-called '*référé liberté*' cases— that is, certain urgent cases bearing on fundamental rights and liberties—is competent to rely on the protections which flow from the EU legal order in protecting fundamental rights. Safeguarding the respect of the 'fundamental liberties which the legal order of the European Union attaches to the status of being a Union citizen', the judge sitting in '*référé liberté*' cases will take the measures necessary to stop serious and manifest breaches caused by an administrative decision to 'the rights conferred by the legal order of the European Union'.[102]

---

[98] Conseil d'État, 29 December 1978, *Darmont*.
[99] Conseil d'État, 18 June 2008, *Gestas*.
[100] Conseil d'État, 30 Decmber 2002, *Ministre de l'aménagement du territoire et de l'environnement c/ Carminati*.
[101] Juge des référés du Conseil d'État, 16 June 2010, *Diakite*.
[102] Juge des référés du Conseil d'État, 9 December 2014, *Mme Pouabem*.

In its judgment in *Kandyrine*, the Conseil d'État had to decide on how a domestic court should resolve the question of alleged incompatibility of international treaties. Having satisfied itself that the two treaties can indeed be relied on in domestic law, it is for the court to endeavour to reconcile their provisions, if necessary by interpreting them against the backdrop of constitutional principle and principles of public order. If, having tried this, the court finds that the provisions remain incompatible, it is for the domestic court:

> to apply the international standard in the field of which the disputed administrative decision has sought to be placed and for the application of which this decision has been taken and, accordingly, to dismiss the ground of its incompatibility with the other international standard put forward, without prejudice to the consequences which may result in regard to the involvement of the responsibility of the State both in international and national law.

But the Conseil d'État stressed that the framework it had drawn up in respect of general international law did not apply in respect of an integrated legal order such as that of the European Union.[103]

Generally the Conseil d'État has defined the role of the administrative courts on the basis of the rule according to which the domestic courts are judges 'of ordinary law for the application of Community law'.[104] It flows from this point of departure that the domestic courts must secure the effectiveness of EU law by all means at their disposal.[105]

The Tribunal des Conflits, too, has accorded a special role to EU law. Deciding on the obligations incumbent on the two judicial orders—the ordinary courts and the administrative courts—to defer the decision in a case in order to make a preliminary reference to the other judicial order, it took the view that the superiority of treaties over statutes,

---

[103] Assemblée plenière of the Conseil d'État, 23 December 2011, *Kandyrine*.
[104] Conseil d'État, 30 October 2009, *Mme Perreux*.
[105] Conseil d'État, 14 May 2010, *Rujovic*.

as set out by Article 55 of the Constitution, has no application in the matter, even when the case concerns the compatibility of an administrative act with an international treaty. But the Tribunal des Conflits has blunted the impact of this approach, epitomized by its decision in *Septfonds*,[106] by holding that a preliminary reference is not necessary 'when it is manifest, against the background of well-established case-law, that the contestation may be accommodated by the court before which the case was first brought'.[107] This does not, however, apply in respect of 'the special case of the European Union'.[108] The Tribunal des Conflits began by pointing out that the respect for EU law 'constitutes an obligation, by virtue of the Treaty on European Union, the Treaty on the Functioning of the European Union, and by application of Article 88-1 of the Constitution'.[109] Having underscored that, in line with *Simmenthal*,[110] the principle of effectiveness introduces a duty on the domestic courts, when applying provisions of EU law, 'to give full effect to those provisions, if necessary by refusing of its own motion to apply any conflicting provision of national legislation',[111] the Tribunal des Conflits held that if, in a case involving a difficulty of interpretation of EU law, the ordinary courts make a preliminary reference to the Court of Justice, they must conclude in the matter without making a reference also to the administrative courts, if what is at issue is the conformity with EU law of an administrative act.[112] This jurisprudence has been applied by the Conseil d'État, which has relied on the same principle when the validity of an act of private law character is contested before the administrative courts against the requirements of EU law.[113] The Cour de cassation, too, applies

---

[106] Tribunal des Conflits, 16 June 1923, *Septfonds*.
[107] Tribunal des Conflits, 17 October 2011, *Préfet de la région Bretagne SCEA du Chéneau*.
[108] ibid.   [109] ibid.
[110] Case 106/77 *Simmenthal* ECLI:EU:C:1978:49 at [24].
[111] Tribunal des Conflits, 17 October 2011, *Préfet de la région Bretagne SCEA du Chéneau*.
[112] ibid.   [113] Conseil d'État, 23 March 2012, *Fédération Sud Santé*.

the framework set out by the Tribunal des Conflits.[114] Both judicial orders thus have full jurisdiction in respect of the application of EU law, with the one exception concerning preliminary references to the Court of Justice. The domestic mechanism of preliminary references as between the judicial orders thus accords to EU law a special status which, although it 'did not itself invite it',[115] finds itself elevated in its singularity.

3. SHARED GUIDING PRINCIPLES

Numerous time-hallowed principles found in the law of the Member States have been elevated to the European level, particularly in the jurisprudence of the Court of Justice that recognizes general principles of Community law on the basis of the shared constitutional traditions of the Member States. Principles which have been affirmed in the first place in one State and recognized at the level of the European Union are thus generalized across the other countries. They often resonate in the law of the European Convention on Human Rights. These shared principles are derived from this synthesis, through cross-fertilization and reciprocal exchange. They structure the European legal system. Four of them make up the keystone of the construct of European law—these are the principles of equality, proportionality, subsidiarity, and legal certainty.

Equality and Non-discrimination

In France equality is at the very heart of the Republican ideal. In Article 1 the Declaration of the Rights of Man and of the Citizen of 1789 proclaims that '[m]en are born and remain free and equal in

---

[114] Cour de cassation, 1ère civile, 24 April 2013, *Commune de Sancoins et Syndicat mixte du parc des Grivelles*.
[115] F Donnat, 'Chronique' in *Dalloz*, December 2011.

rights', and Article 6 affirms that the law 'must be the same for all, whether it protects or punishes'. The principle of equality applies to different contexts, to the incidence of the law, taxation, public office, civil service, and public services. It 'governs the functioning of public services', according to the 1951 judgment of the Conseil d'État in *Société des concerts du Conservatoire*,[116] which in terms characterized equality as a general principle of law.

Given pride of place in the constitutions of numerous European countries, the principle of equality is a principle shared by all. Within Community law it manifests itself in the first place as non-discrimination on the basis of nationality. All kinds of discrimination, direct or indirect, that might stymie the free interplay of exchanges are prohibited. On the basis of this principally economic and commercial acknowledgment, the ambit of the principle of equality has broadened to include fundamental rights as well. The Court of Justice has held that it 'is one of the fundamental principles of Community law'.[117] The Court's review is particularly searching in respect of the equality between men and women[118] and in respect of age discrimination.[119] Directives contribute to directing Community law towards fighting discrimination, such as Directive 2000/43 of 29 June 2000 implementing the principle of equal treatment between persons irrespective of racial or ethnic origin[120] and Directive 2000/78 of 27 November 2000 establishing a general framework for equal treatment in employment and occupation.[121] This trend is crowned in Article 21(1) of the Charter of Fundamental Rights, which prohibits:

[a]ny discrimination based on any ground such as sex, race, colour, ethnic or social origin, genetic features, language, religion or belief,

---

[116] Conseil d'État, 9 March 1951, *Société des concerts du Conservatoire*.
[117] Cases 117/76 and 16/77 *Ruckdeschel* ECLI:EU:C:1977:160 at [7].
[118] Case C–366/99 *Griesmar* ECLI:EU:C:2001:648.
[119] Case C–144/04 *Mangold* ECLI:EU:C:2005:709.
[120] [2000] OJ L180/22.   [121] [2000] OJ L303/16.

political or any other opinion, membership of a national minority, property, birth, disability, age or sexual orientation.

These terms are close to those of Article 14 of the European Convention on Human Rights. Although that article concerns only the absence of discrimination in the enjoyment of the rights and freedoms guaranteed by the Convention, the European Court of Human Rights has conferred on it an autonomous meaning by prohibiting any form of discrimination. Protocol 12,[122] which entered into force on 1 April 2005, extends to the countries which have ratified it this jurisprudence by affirming that 'any right set forth by law' shall be secured without discrimination.[123]

The principle of equality does not mean that different treatment cannot apply to different situations. But, here as in other connections, the difference in treatment must be rationally connected to the different situations and it must respond to compelling grounds of the general interest attaching to the public services in question. This jurisprudence, relied on by the Conseil d'État,[124] is shared by the Conseil constitutionnel, which on numerous occasions has held that 'the principle of equality does not prohibit the legislator from regulating different situations differently, nor does it prohibit derogations from the principle of equality for reasons of general interest, so long as, in both situations, the resulting difference of treatment is rationally connected with the object of the statute'.[125]

This conception of equality is also shared by other European courts. The constitutional courts of, in particular, Austria and Italy jealously protect the right to equality, characterized by the Austrian Constitutional Court as a 'metarule'. The German Federal Constitutional Court follows a similar approach. For example, it set

---

[122] Convention for the Protection of Human Rights (Protocol No 12), 4 November 2000, ETS 177.
[123] ibid Art 1(1).   [124] Conseil d'État, 10 May 1974, *Denoyes & Chorques*.
[125] See eg Decision No 2015–517 QPC of 22 January 2016 at [16].

aside the Act to Amend the Hamburg Act on the Protection against Passive Smoking,[126] which adopted more restrictive measures for eating and drinking establishments than for drinking establishments, since no objective difference of situation between the two categories of establishment justified such a difference of treatment.[127]

The law of the European Union has adopted the same principle of equality, conceptualized as the absence of discrimination. It adds, however, an additional requirement, that of not treating different situations in the same way,[128] whereas in the view of the Conseil d'État[129] and the Conseil constitutionnel[130] the principle of equality does not necessitate different treatment of persons who find themselves in different situations.

When it is based on achieving a sufficiently important objective, positive discrimination is not contrary to the principle of equality. The general interest attaching to children being able to go to music school, whatever the financial situation of their parents, thus authorizes a local council to vary the registration fees of the council conservatory according to the salaries of the parents.[131] Similarly a statute may authorize the Paris Institute of Political Studies (Sciences Po) to open a special access scheme by offering special agreements to schools in certain prioritized zones, on the basis of the 'constitutional requirement of equal access to education', so long as the candidates are recruited on the basis of objective criteria, taking account of their level of achievement and their abilities.[132]

---

[126] Gesetz zur Änderung des Hamburgischen Passivraucherschutzgesetze 15 December 2009, GVBl p 506.

[127] BVerfGE 130, 131 *Hamburgisches Passivraucherschutzgesetz.*

[128] Case C–394/96 *Brown v Rentokil* ECLI:EU:C:1998:331; Case C–148/02 *Garcia Avello* ECLI:EU:C:2003:539.

[129] Conseil d'État, 28 March 1997, *Société Baxter*; Conseil d'État, 2 October 2003, *Rolland.*

[130] Decision No 2003–489 of 29 December 2003 at [37]; Decision No 2012–654 of 9 August 2012 at [19].

[131] Conseil d'État, 29 December 1997, *Commune de Gennevillers.*

[132] Decision No 2001–450 of 11 July 2001 at [31]–[33].

At the European level, the Directives of 29 June and 27 November 2000 similarly authorize 'the maintenance or adoption of measures intended to prevent or compensate for disadvantages' stemming from discrimination. Within the framework of its work against discrimination the European Union itself has engaged in 'affirmative action'.

Proportionality

The principle of proportionality originated in German law.[133] It appeared in the *Kreuzberg* judgment of the Supreme Court of Prussia of 14 June 1882;[134] commenting in 1912 on the judgment, the German jurist Fritz Fleiner wrote that '[t]he police must not shoot sparrows with cannons'.[135]

Without using the word proportionality, the Conseil d'État in France developed a standard of review of police measures which was similarly inspired. The administrative courts would conduct a searching review of the rational connection of the means relied on to achieve the requirement of public order. In a decision from 1909, *Abbé Olivier*, the Conseil d'État annulled a mayoral decree prohibiting religious funeral processions on public highways, by reverting to the law of 9 December 1905 relative to the separation of Church and State which aimed to 'respect as far as possible local customs and traditions and … interfere with them only to the extent that it is strictly necessary in the interest of keeping public order'. In his conclusions in the proceeding, *Commissaire du gouvernement* Chardenet explained the spirit in which, in his view, the Conseil d'État ought to perform its review:

> You are in a fashion called upon to perform the role of the hierarchical superior to the administrative authorities; you must examine

---

[133] Cf however the early UK precedents brought to light in P Craig, 'Proportionality and Judicial Review: A UK Historical Perspective' in *General Principles of Law: European and Comparative Perspectives* (Hart 2017).

[134] *Entscheidungen des Preußischen Oberverwaltungsgerichts Vol IX* (Heymann 1883) 364.

[135] F Fleiner, *Institutionen des deutschen Verwaltungsrecht* (JCB Mohr 1912) 354 ('Die Polizei soll nicht mit Kanonen auf Spatzen schießen.').

what is the limit of the duties of the mayor and ascertain whether the purported reliance on the State's police powers was exercised in the interest of the maintenance of public order.[136]

The conclusions of *Commissaire du gouvernement* Corneille in the 1917 judgment *Baldy* followed in the same vein:

> In order to determine the extent of the police powers in the context of a specific case, it must in the first place be recalled that the State's police powers are always restrictions on the liberties of individuals; that the body of liberties of the citizen is the point of departure of our public law; that the Declaration of the Rights of Man is, implicitly or explicitly, referred to in the preamble of all the Republican constitutions. Finally it must be remembered that every public law dispute must, in order to comply with the general principles of law, begin with the realization that liberty is the rule; police restrictions, the exception.[137]

The 1933 judgment in *Benjamin* affirmed these principles by annulling a decree of the mayor of Nevers, which had prohibited Mr René Benjamin, a literary critic close to the extreme right, from giving a lecture in the city on 'two comic authors: Courteline and Sacha Guitry'. At the general level, the judgment shows that: 'if it falls to the mayor ... to take measures of public order; he must balance the exercise of his powers with the respect for the freedom of assembly'. In the circumstances, the Conseil d'État determined that:

> the contingency that there should be disturbances, as alleged by the mayor of Nevers, did not present a degree of gravity such that he could not, without prohibiting the lecture, maintain order by exercising the necessary police powers.[138]

---

[136] Conseil d'État, 19 February 1909, *Abbé Olivier* (conclusions: Chardenet).
[137] Conseil d'État, 17 August 1917, *Baldy* (conclusions: Corneille).
[138] Conseil d'État, 19 Mai 1917, *Benjamin* (conclusions: Michel).

It falls in the first place to the authority in question to guarantee the enjoyment of civil liberties, especially as fundamental a liberty as the freedom of assembly. Only when the means at his or her disposal are not equal to the task of maintaining public order may a restrictive measure be resorted to.

Police measures are legal only to the extent that they are necessary. That means that the administrative authority needs to verify that the measures are adequate in the circumstances. General and absolute prohibitions—blanket bans—do not satisfy the requirements of proportionality. It is by confronting, in each particular case, the extent of the restrictions of civil liberties with the imperatives of public order that the authority and, if need be, the administrative courts, will determine which restrictions are legally permissible. Thus, for example, the Conseil d'État examined, in the context of so-called minors' curfews, from which hour of the day and where a mayor may, as a function of local circumstances, prohibit minors from going outside without being accompanied.[139] Respect for human dignity often features as a reason of public order justifying the intervention relying on police powers.[140]

The principles on which the case-law of the administrative courts is based have been given constitutional imprimatur, as the Conseil constitutionnel has relied on them in its review of the conformity with the Constitution of statutes which restrict the exercise of civil liberties.

The decision of the Conseil constitutionnel of 12 January 1977 relating to the law on vehicle searches,[141] which characterized individual liberty as a fundamental principle recognized by the laws of the Republic, marked the beginning of a jurisprudence of which the result is that, for statutes too, liberty is the rule; police restrictions, the

---

[139] Conseil d'État, 2 August 2001, *Préfet de Vaucluse*; Conseil d'État, 10 August 2001, *Commune d'Yerres*.

[140] Conseil d'État, 27 October 1995, *Commune de Morsang-sur-Orge*; Juge des référés du Conseil d'État, 9 January 2014, *Ministre de l'intérieur c/ Société les Productions de la Plume et M. M'Bala M'Bala*.

[141] Decision No 76–75 of 12 January 1977.

exception. The Conseil constitutionnel relied on these principles in its successive decisions on stop and searches,[142] as well as in its decision of 18 January 1995 on video surveillance.[143] It generally takes the view that statutory restrictions of civil liberties 'must be rationally connected to the objective, necessary, and proportionate in relation to the objective sought attained'.[144]

It is for the legislator, as it is for any administrative authority, to reconcile constitutional principles and the protection of public order, which has been characterized as a constitutional value. The Conseil constitutionnel has thus observed that:

> it is incumbent on the legislator to reconcile, on the one hand, the prevention of offences against public order and the search for perpetrators of crime, both of which are necessary for the safeguarding of constitutional rights and principles, and, on the other hand, the enjoyment of constitutionally guaranteed liberties, of which the right to free movement, the right to privacy, and individual liberty are ones.[145]

This reconciliation will, in each case, be carried out with a view to whether the measure was appropriate; it is an example of proportionality.

Conceived in Germany and illustrated in France, the principle of proportionality has spread through the body of domestic law. In Italy the Consiglio di Stato has characterized it as a general principle, on an equal footing with the principle of equality.[146] Even a legal system as resistant to principles as the United Kingdom has adopted it.[147]

---

[142] Decision No 80–127 of 20 January 1981; Decision No 86–211 of 26 August 1986; Decision No 93–323 of 5 August 1993.

[143] Decision No 94–352 of 18 January 1995.

[144] See eg Decision No 2013–367 QPC of 14 February 2014 at [6].

[145] Decision No 2003–467 of 13 March 2003; Decision 2005–532 of 19 January 2006.

[146] Consiglio di Stato, 21 March 1972; Consiglio di Stato, 23 April 1974.

[147] See P Craig, 'Proportionality and Judicial Review: A UK Historical Perspective' in *General Principles of Law: European and Comparative Perspectives* (Hart 2017).

Lord Diplock illustrated the principle thus: '[i]n plain English, "you must not use a steam hammer to crack a nut, if a nutcracker would do".[148] The Appellate Committee of the House of Lords expressly relied on the principle of proportionality.[149] Similarly the Supreme Court has held, in connection with the requirements of Article 8 of the European Convention on Human Rights, that the ban on the entry for settlement of foreign spouses or civil partners unless both parties were aged twenty-one or over, contained in paragraph 277 of the Immigration Rules,[150] was in breach of the principle of proportionality.[151] The Supreme Court now regularly refers to the principle of proportionality.[152]

Since its 1970 ruling in *Internationale Handelsgesellschaft* the Court of Justice has characterized as general principles of Community law principles as common as proportionality.[153] The Advocate General, Alain Dutheillet de Lamothe, in his conclusions in that case invited the Court to reaffirm the principle of proportionality on the basis of 'the fundamental right ... that the individual should not have his freedom of action limited beyond the degree necessary for the general interest'.[154] In the jurisprudence it has become one of the most important principles of Community law: 'The principle of proportionality is a fundamental principle of Community law whose observance the Court must assure'.[155] It 'requires that measures implemented

---

[148] *R v Goldstein* [1983] 1 WLR 151, 155.

[149] *R (Daly) v Secretary of State for the Home Department* [2001] 2 AC 532 (Lord Steyn); *R v Shayler* [2003] 1 AC 247 at [57]–[59] (Lord Hope); *Huang v Secretary of State for the Home Department* [2007] 2 AC 167 at [19] (Lord Bingham).

[150] Immigration Rules 1994 (HC 395).

[151] *R (Quila) v Secretary of State for the Home Department* [2012] 1 AC 621 at [45] (Lord Wilson).

[152] *Bank Mellat v Her Majesty's Treasury* [2013] UKSC 38, [2014] AC 700; *Pham v Secretary of State for the Home Department* [2015] UKSC 19, [2015] 1 WLR 1591; *R (on the Application of Keyu) v Secretary of State for Foreign and Commonwealth Affairs* [2015] UKSC 69, [2015] 3 WLR 1665.

[153] Case 11–70 *Internationale Handelsgesellschaft* ECLI:EU:C:1970:114 at [4].

[154] Opinion of Mr Advocate General Dutheillet de Lamothe—Case 11–70 *Internationale Handelsgesellschaft* ECLI:EU:C:1970:100 p 1147.

[155] Opinion of Mr Advocate General Fennelly—Case C–217/99 *Commission v Belgium* ECLI:EU:C:2000:355 at [35]; Case 182/84 *Miro* ECLI:EU:C:1985:470 at [14].

through Community provisions should be appropriate for attaining the objective pursued and must not go beyond what is necessary to achieve it'.[156]

The European Convention on Human Rights, too, has made the principle of proportionality one of the fundamentals of the framework on which it relies in the safeguarding of rights and liberties. Whereas the right to life, the prohibition of torture and inhuman and degrading treatment, and of slavery are absolute rights, the other rights of the Convention may be subject to restrictions which are 'in accordance with the law' and 'necessary in a democratic society' in the interests of, especially, national security, public safety, for the prevention of disorder or crime, for the protection of health or morals, or for the protection of the rights and freedoms of others. The final step is ascertaining whether a fair balance has been struck between the interests of the individual and those of society. In this regard the States have a certain margin of appreciation, within the bounds of proportionality and under the supervision of the Court. 'The principle of proportionality, based on the requirement of rational connection between a legitimate aim and the means relied on for its achievement, is at the heart of the review of the margin of appreciation', Professor Frédéric Sudre has written.[157] In that sense it joins hands with the principle of subsidiarity.

Subsidiarity

Unlike the principles of equality and proportionality, the principle of subsidiarity had scarcely manifested itself legally until the Treaty of Maastricht made it a part of European law.

The principle of subsidiarity provides that the responsibility of public action should lie with the capable authority that is the closest

---

[156] Case C–491/01 *British American Tobacco* ECLI:EU:C:2002:741 at [122].

[157] F Sudre and others, *Les grands arrêts de la Cour européenne des droits de l'homme* (2nd edn, Presses universitaires de France 2015) 69.

to the citizen. The ancient origins of the principle are held to originate in the thought of Aristotle, in the theology of Thomas Aquinas (1226–1274), and the philosophy of the German jurist Johannes Althusius (1556–1617), author of the work *Politica* (1603). It inspired the social doctrine of the Catholic Church, as expressed in the Encyclicals *Rerum novarum* of Leo XIII in 1891 and *Quadragesimo Anno* of Pius XI in 1931.[158]

In federal States, the division of powers between the federation and the federated communities follows the idea of subsidiarity. This is implicitly the case in Germany in respect of the division of competences between the federal State and the *Länder*.[159] But it is principally under British influence that, with the Treaty of Maastricht, the principle of subsidiarity appeared in the law of the European Union, the Treaty emphasizing in its preamble that it is the foundation of 'an ever closer union among the peoples of Europe, in which decisions are taken as closely as possible to the citizen in accordance with the principle of subsidiarity'. This formula is reaffirmed in the preamble of the Treaty on European Union, which provides, in Article 5, that:

[u]nder the principle of subsidiarity, in areas which do not fall within its exclusive competence, the Union shall act only if and in so far as the objectives of the proposed action cannot be sufficiently achieved by the Member States, either at central level or at regional and local level, but can rather, by reason of the scale or effects of the proposed action, be better achieved at Union level.

Emphasized by EU law, the principle of subsidiarity is also taken up by domestic law. On the occasion of the revision necessary for the ratification of the Treaty of Maastricht, it was inscribed into Article

---

[158] See J Bell, 'Subsidiarity in English Law' (forthcoming).

[159] See eg T Oppermann, 'Subsidiarität im Sinne des Deutschen Grundgesetzes' in KN Nörr and T Oppermann (eds), *Subsidiarität: Idee und Wirklichkeit* (JCB Mohr 1997) 215.

23 of the German Basic Law. In 2001 it was mentioned in terms in Article 118 of the Italian Constitution, as a principle of the division of competences between the State, the regions, the provinces, and the communes.

In France, too, its entry into positive law came about within the framework of territorial organization. It was mentioned for the first time, in the year of the ratification of the Maastricht Treaty, by law of 6 February 1992 on the territorial administration of the Republic and by decree of 28 March 1992, the charter of devolution.[160] With the revision of 28 March 2003, subsidiarity was given pride of place, in Article 72 of the Constitution, of which the second sentence provides that: 'Territorial communities may take decisions in all matters arising under powers that can best be exercised at their level.'

Though its import is different, subsidiarity is at the heart of the structure of the rights constituting the European Convention on Human Rights. It is in the first place for the State and its courts to guarantee respect for the rights guaranteed by the Convention. The European Court of Human Rights has underscored repeatedly that: 'the machinery of protection established by the Convention is subsidiary to the national systems safeguarding human rights.'[161] From a procedural point of view, subsidiarity is expressed through the exhaustion of domestic remedies; in terms of the substance of the law, it is manifested in the national margin of appreciation. Adopted soon after the Brighton Conference in April 2012, Protocol 15 underscored the importance of subsidiarity, by envisaging the addition to the preamble of the European Convention of a recital which affirms:

> that the High Contracting Parties, in accordance with the principle of subsidiarity, have the primary responsibility to secure the rights and freedoms defined in this Convention and the Protocols

---

[160] Decree of 7 May 2015 enacted, in the same vein, a new charter of devolution.
[161] *Handyside v United Kingdom* (1979–80) 1 EHRR 737, (1976) 58 ILR 150 at [48]; *Belgian Linguistic Case (No 2)* (1968) 1 EHRR 252, (1968) 45 ILR at [10].

thereto, and that in doing so they enjoy a margin of appreciation, subject to the supervisory jurisdiction of the European Court of Human Rights.[162]

Although it takes the view that it is charged with the supervision of the respect of the principle of subsidiarity in the context of EU law,[163] the Court of Justice has not had occasion to set aside for example secondary legislation on the basis of breach of subsidiarity. The principle is strongly emphasized by the Treaty of Lisbon, which in Article 5(3) gives national parliaments the role of ensuring compliance with the principle. Upstream the national parliaments, or the chambers of which they are made up, may issue reasoned opinions on the conformity with the principle of subsidiarity of a European legislative proposal. Such an opinion is addressed to the presidents of the European Parliament, of the Council, and of the Commission. Depending on their number, these opinions have consequences for the European decision-making process. Further downstream, the parliamentary assemblies have the option of bringing a case before the Court of Justice against the legislative proposal, on the grounds of alleged violation of the principle of subsidiarity. In France the intervention of Parliament in this connection is fleshed out by Article 88-6 of the Constitution which, in accordance with a rule similar to the one applying to the Conseil constitutionnel, sets out the ways in which the National Assembly or the Senate, through sixty deputies or senators, may institute proceedings before the Court of Justice.

These rules reveal the political importance of the principle of subsidiarity. Even if, under the law of the European Union, the detailed character of certain acts of secondary law and, within the framework of the European Convention on Human Rights, the at times pointillist case-law of the Court may both seem to depart from the principle,

---

[162] Art 1, CETS 213—Human Rights (Protocol No 15) 24 June 2013.
[163] Case C–154/04 *Nutri-Link* ECLI:EU:C:2005:449; Case C–58/08 *Vodafone* ECLI:EU:C:2010:321.

subsidiarity appears more and more as a fundamental principle for the co-existence of European and domestic law. It is indispensable if the law of the European Union and that of the European Convention are to remain at their supranational level, without getting lost in the details which would make them both ineffective and unsustainable. It alone can give full effect to the principle which makes domestic courts the prime movers of European law and which gives them the role of courts generally competent to decide in matters relating to the application of the law of the European Union. It establishes between States, the European Union, and the Council of Europe bonds which the States, federal as well as unitary ones, increasingly apply to their relations with their own devolved communities. It thus operates to conciliate the requirements of reconciliation and the imperatives of diversity.

Legal Certainty

The first and major goal of a legal system, legal certainty implies qualitative requirements: clarity, stability, and predictability. Legal certainty is both distinct from and closely related to the concept of legitimate expectations which, on the basis of a more subjective approach, presupposes a reasonable assurance in respect of the commitment. In both cases, what is at issue is guaranteeing a legal order which satisfies the requirements of clarity and solidity.

Although they have not been given expression in the EU Treaties, the principles of legal certainty and legitimate expectations have been emphasized strongly by the Court of Justice, which already at an early stage characterized legal certainty as a general principle of Community law.[164] The Court conceives of the principle of legal certainty as a 'fundamental requirement' of the Community legal order.[165] Indeed it considers that the principle of the protection of

---

[164] Case 13–61 *Bosch* ECLI:EU:C:1962:11 p 52.
[165] Case 52–69 *JR Geigy AG v Commission* ECLI:EU:C:1972:73 at [21].

legitimate expectations 'is one of the fundamental principles of the Community'.[166]

Legal certainty and legitimate expectations originated in German law. Although the principles were not conceptualized as such in French law, the concerns they address had been recognized from an early point in French law too. Those concerns have given rise to the rules regarding the publication of laws and regulations, inspired the principle of non-retroactivity, and they explain a number of series of cases, especially within the field of revocation of administrative decisions, acquired rights, and unfulfilled promises.

Whilst it has been emphasized in Community law, in French law legal certainty would take on an all the greater role as it was seen to be a reaction to the increasing complexity and instability of the law. The Conseil d'État's public report of 1991—in which the Conseil d'État decried what it saw as 'normative inflation'—had the title *On legal certainty*.[167] In particular, it observed that 'when the law speaks idly, citizens lend it only a distracted ear', or in the original: '*quand le droit bavarde, le citoyen ne lui prête qu'une oreille distraite*'.[168] Fifteen years later, having noted that the inflation continued unabatedly, the Conseil d'État chose as the title of the general discussions of its public report of 2006 *Legal Certainty and the Complexity of the Law*.[169] Through its 2006 judgment in *Société KPMG*, the Conseil d'État made the principles of legal certainty a part of the domestic legal order, by characterizing it as a general principle of law.[170] The judgment in *Société Techna* of the same year observed that the principle is 'recognized both in domestic law and by the legal order of the European Union'.[171] In the

---

[166] Case C–112/80 *Dürbeck* ECLI:EU:C:1981:94 at [48].
[167] *Rapport public du Conseil d'État 1991: De la sécurité juridique* (Conseil d'État 1991).
[168] ibid 15.
[169] *Rapport public du Conseil d'État 2006: Sécurité juridique et complexité du droit* (Conseil d'État 2006).
[170] Conseil d'État, 24 March 2006, *Société KPGM*.
[171] Conseil d'État, 27 October 2006, *Société Techna*.

triage of requests for priority preliminary rulings on constitutionality, the Conseil d'État will review claims under the heading of breach of legal certainty, by attaching the latter to the guarantee of rights proclaimed by Article 16 of the Declaration of the Rights of Man 1789.[172]

The same step has not yet been made in respect of legitimate expectations, which the Conseil d'État thus applies only in the field of EU law.[173] It is true, however, that the purchase given to the principle of legal certainty, which according to *KPMG* requires that new regulations must lay down the necessary transitional provisions such that new regulations cannot apply immediately to contracts which have already been concluded, overlaps with aspects of legitimate expectations.

Without being willing to characterize legitimate expectations[174] or legal certainty as constitutional principles, the Conseil constitutionnel has drawn inspiration from the concerns underlying the two doctrines.

Whereas it admits that non-repressive laws may contain retroactive provisions, the Conseil constitutionnel requires that a general interest of sufficient weight exist for a breach of legally concluded contracts or legally acquired positions to be justified.[175] In terms which are close to the European principles of legal certainty and legitimate expectations, the Conseil constitutionnel had held that the legislator:

> may not, without a sufficiently important object based on the general interest, violate legally acquired positions nor compromise the effects which may legitimately be expected in connection with such positions.[176]

---

[172] Conseil d'État, 21 January 2015, *EURL 2B*. Art 16 of the Declaration of the Rights of Man 1789 provides in pertinent part: 'Any society in which no provision is made for guaranteeing rights ... has no Constitution.'

[173] Conseil d'État 5 March 1999, *Rouquette*; Conseil d'État, 9 Mai 2001, *Entreprise personnelle de transport Freymuth*.

[174] Decision No 97–391 of 7 November 1997.

[175] Decision No 2002–465 of 13 January 2003.

[176] Decision No 2013–682 of 19 December 2013.

It has characterized the accessibility and intelligibility of the law—not all that far removed from legal certainty—as an objective of constitutional value.[177] Generally, the Conseil constitutionnel has observed that the 'quality of the law' is a principle of constitutional value, which requires that the legislator:

> adopt provisions sufficiently precise and non-equivocal wording, with a view to allowing citizens to defend against interpretations which are contrary to the Constitution or against the risk of arbitrariness.[178]

A statute of 'excessive complexity' will be held to breach the 'guarantee of rights', as it flows from Article 16 of the Declaration of the Rights of Man 1789.[179] The wording is very similar to the definition of legal certainty.

Legal certainty finds a place, too, in the law of the European Convention on Human Rights. It leads to a requirement of precision and predictability of the law,[180] a necessary attribute of the 'rule of law', which the Convention regards as 'one of the fundamental principles of a democratic society'.[181] It limits the ways in which a statute may have retroactive effects. In criminal matters no retroactivity is possible. This prohibition applies to preventative detention, as the European Court of Human Rights observed in connection with a German statute, by referring in its decision[182] to that of the Conseil constitutionnel of 21 February 2008 on a similar French statute.[183] In other fields, the Court has taken a firm line on retroactive legislation

---

[177] Decision No 99–421 of 16 December 1999.
[178] Decision No 98–401 of 10 June 1998; Decision No 99–411 of 16 June 1999; Decision No 2004–500 of 29 July 2004.
[179] Decision No 2005–530 of 29 December 2005.
[180] *Sunday Times v United Kingdom* (1979–80) 2 EHRR 245 at [49]; *Hentrich v France* (1994) 18 EHRR 440 at [42].
[181] *Brogan v United Kindom* (1989) 11 EHRR 117 at [58].
[182] *M v Germany* (2010) 51 EHRR 41.
[183] Decision No 2008–562 of 21 February 2008.

and, in particular, on laws designed to legalize existing practices, which only compelling grounds of the general interest can justify.[184] These requirements were taken up by both the Cour de cassation[185] and the Conseil d'État.[186] The Conseil constitutionnel, too, has adopted the terminology of the Strasbourg Court, by requiring that a statute designed to legalize existing practices be justified by compelling grounds of the general interest. Within the field of criminal law, in order for a law to be in compliance with the European Convention it must also be sufficiently precise and predictable.[187]

By posing demanding requirements both at the European and the domestic level, legal certainty has consequences also for the courts themselves and for the temporal application of their judgments.

In the interest of promoting legal certainty, the Treaty of Rome gave the Court of Justice the option of modulating the temporal effect of its decisions annulling acts of secondary law. In its jurisprudence, the Court went further, placing temporal restriction on its decisions both in requests for interpretation[188] and for pleas for illegality.[189] Several European constitutional and supreme courts, especially the Italian Corte costituzionale, have followed in the same vein.

Similar concerns explain the important judicial development which came about in France in the decision of the Conseil d'État in *Association AC!*[190] Although the retroactive effect of a judgment annulling an administrative act as being ultra vires ('*annulation pour excès de pouvoir*') is the rule, exceptions can be made to this rule if the court finds that the retroactive effect of the annulment would have manifestly disproportionate consequences. The

---

[184] *Zielinski v France* (2001) 31 EHRR 19.
[185] Cour de cassation, 24 April 2001, *Association 'Etre enfant au Chesnay'*.
[186] Conseil d'État, 23 June 2004, *Société laboratoires Genevrier*.
[187] Cour de cassation, Crim, 16 January 2001 and 20 February 2001.
[188] Case 43–75 *Defrenne* ECLI:EU:C:1976:39.
[189] Case 138/79 *Roquette* ECLI:EU:C:1980:249.
[190] Conseil d'État, 11 May 2004, *Association AC!*

administrative courts may also decide that all or some of the effects of the act are definitive, or order that the annulment does not take effect until a later date determined by the court. In connection with the constitutional revision of 23 July 2008, this jurisprudence inspired the definition of powers of the Conseil constitutionnel when an introduction of priority preliminary rulings on constitutionality is brought before it. According to the rules codified in Article 62 of the Constitution, the provision declared unconstitutional by the Conseil constitutionnel is repealed as of the publication of the decision, or at a later time determined the Conseil constitutionnel in its decision; furthermore it determines the conditions and limits according to which the effects produced by the provision may be challenged.

Beyond the effects of annulments, legal certainty imposes on the courts certain obligations of stability—and thus of predictability—of case-law. True, as the European Court of Human Rights has observed, the requirements of legal certainty and of legitimate expectations should not exclude jurisprudential developments; the evolution of case-law is a part of the judicial function and legal certainty and the protection of legitimate expectations 'do not confer an acquired right to consistency of case-law'.[191] But it has also emphasized that, when they develop their case-law, domestic supreme courts must explain the developments by sufficiently precise grounds justifying the departure.[192] For reasons connected to legal certainty, the Conseil d'État and the Cour de cassation have furthermore modulated the temporal effect of their jurisprudential departures in cases where the change has a bearing on the right to an effective remedy.[193]

---

[191] *Sahin v Turkey* (2012) 54 EHRR 20 at [58]; *Unédic v France* (unreported) App No 20153/04 judgment 18 December 2008 at [74].

[192] *Atanasovski v Macedonia* (2010) 28 BHRC 63 at [37]–[38].

[193] Conseil d'État, 16 July 2007, *Société Tropic travaux signalisation*; 6 June 2008, *Conseil départemental de l'ordre des chirurgiens-dentistes de Paris*; Cour de cassation, 21 December 2006 and 11 June 2009.

By means of a mutually defined hierarchy of norms, of the special role of the integrated legal order of the EU, and of certain shared guiding principles, European and domestic law are increasingly closely connected. Their good relationship is founded, to a large extent, on a body of case-law which the European and domestic courts are fashioning together.

5

The Independence and Interdependence of Judges

Neither soldiers nor ambassadors but judges.
—Sabino Cassese, *When Legal Orders Collide* (2010)

Profound differences exist between the judicial systems of the various European countries. These variations concern, in particular, whether or not the system has a constitutional court, whether there is unity (as in eg the United Kingdom) or duality (as in eg France) between the judicial orders, and the status of the judges. On these varied points there is, however, a measure of convergence. This convergence is reinforced by the role that European law confers on the courts. By the role that it accords to the two European courts—the Court of Justice of the European Union and the European Court of Human Rights—and by the dialogue it invites between these two courts and the domestic courts, European law operates to expand the authority of judges in Europe. Professor Sabino Cassese, former member of the Italian constitutional court, Corte costituzionale, observed that in tomorrow's Europe there will no longer be a need for warriors, or diplomats; but there will be a need for judges: '[n]either soldiers nor ambassadors but judges.'[1]

---

[1] S Cassese, *When Legal Orders Collide: The Role of Courts* (Global Law Press 2010). Towards a European Public Law. First Edition. Bernard Stirn. © Bernard Stirn 2017. Published 2017 by Oxford University Press.

European law requires independence and impartiality of all Europe's judges, all the while demanding that they listen to each other and draw inspiration from one another reciprocally. They are encouraged—to take the phrase coined by French Prime Minister Edgar Faure in 1955 in connection with the relationship he wished would come into being between France and Morocco—to strive for 'independence within interdependence'.

Quite apart from the diversity existing between the different domestic systems, the fundamental trends which are developing have come about under European influence: constitutional law is constitutionalizing; judicial control of the executive is being reinforced; the right to an effective remedy, before an independent and impartial tribunal, is becoming a core value; the dialogue and interaction between courts, and the interdependence amongst them, is becoming reality.

1. THE DEVELOPMENT OF CONSTITUTIONAL LAW

First developed in the case-law of the United States Supreme Court, which at an early point recognized the power of the courts to set aside laws held to be contrary to the Constitution,[2] constitutional law properly so-called was for a long time unknown in Europe.[3] Only Austria, under the influence of Hans Kelsen, gave itself a Constitutional Court in 1920.[4]

The broadening of constitutional justice has also signified a break with traditional approaches. From the wake of the Second World War

---

[2] *Marbury v Madison*, 5 US 137 (1803).

[3] Cf the Norwegian Supreme Court's judgment in *Grev Wedel Jarlsberg v Marinedepartementet* (1866), where the court declared that it would not apply any law that was found to be in conflict with the Constitution: A Bårdsen, 'The Nordic Supreme Courts as Constitutional Courts', lecture given at Vienna, 29–30 October 2015.

[4] See p 81–2 of this volume and eg H Kelsen, *Introduction to the Problems of Legal Theory* (BL Paulson and SL Paulson trs, Clarendon Press 2002 [1934]).

to the fall of the Communist regimes, this came about in successive stages, often connected to the restoration of democracy.

Shaking from its feet the dust of totalitarianism, Italy in 1947 set up a constitutional court, the Corte costituzionale; similarly one of the keystones of the body of new democratic institutions in postwar Germany was the Federal Constitutional Court at Karlsruhe, set up in 1949. During the 1970s the return to democracy in Southern Europe was followed by the creation of constitutional courts by the Greek Constitution of 15 June 1975, the Portuguese Constitution of 2 April 1976, and the Spanish Constitution of 27 December 1978.

Constitutional justice contributed to the move to democracy on the heels of the fall of Communist regimes in Eastern Europe.[5] In 1991 a Russian Constitutional Court replaced the USSR Constitutional Supervision Committee, which had been set up by the Soviet Constitution of 1 December 1988. From 1989 onwards, constitutional courts were installed in Poland, Hungary, Bulgaria, and in the Czech and Slovak Republics; a constitutional court was also created in Bosnia by the Dayton Accords of 1995.[6]

Independently of such historically contingent developments, constitutional law has developed in other European countries too. Having been created by the 1958 Constitution, the French Conseil constitutionnel has over time become a constitutional court worthy of the name, especially after its decision of 16 July 1971, the first instance of the court reviewing the constitutionality of a statute against the background of the principles set out in the preamble of the Constitution.[7] By opening up the seisin of the Conseil constitutionnel to at least sixty deputies or sixty senators, the constitutional revision of 29 October 1974 consolidated this evolution; this in turn was later reinforced by the introduction of the priority preliminary rulings on

---

[5] See M Andenas and others (eds), *Constitutional Reform and International Law in Central and Eastern Europe* (Kluwer 1998) Chs 2–11.

[6] General Framework Agreement for Peace in Bosnia and Herzegovina, 21 November 1995, (1996) ILM 75.

[7] Decision No 71–44 of 16 July 1971.

constitutionality ('*question prioritaire de constitutionnalité*'—QPC)[8] of 23 July 2008. In Belgium a constitutional court was set up in 1980, in the shape of of a Cour d'Arbitrage, which in 2007[9] took the name of Constitutional Court (Cour constitutionnelle and Grondwettelijk Hof in French and Dutch respectively). Constitutional justice—in the sense of a legal system having a designated constitutional court deciding on matters pertaining to the country's constitution—does not obtain in all the European countries. Numerous great democracies, not least the United Kingdom, have decided to do without.[10] Denmark, the Netherlands, and Switzerland, most notably, do not possess a constitutional court.

While it is true that important differences can be found between the constitutional courts of the various European countries, in particular as concerns the designation of their members and the procedures by which applications are brought before them, a number of common features can however be teased out.

Although rules vary as to the requirements of legal qualification, the designation of members of constitutional courts lies in the first place with political authorities, often on the basis of rules adopted with a view to guaranteeing pluralism. Certain nominations are furthermore done by judicial authorities. Long mandates act as a guarantee for independence.

Thus the sixteen Justices of the Federal Constitutional Court at Karlsruhe are elected for twelve non-renewable years, by a majority of two-thirds, half of the judges elected in the Bundestag; the other half, in the Bundesrat. A third of them are elected from members of the federal courts. The fifteen members of the Corte costituzionale, who must come from the ranks of professional judges, are nominated, for a term of nine non-renewable years, by a third party, the President of the Italian Republic. In Spain the twelve members of the Constitutional Court, chosen amongst recognized jurists, are nominated for nine years by the King. Four of them are proposed, by a majority of three-fifths, by the Chamber

---

[8] See p 86 of this volume.   [9] Belgium then becoming a federal State.
[10] Cf P Craig, 'Constitutionalising Constitutional Law: *HS2*' [2014] PL 373.

of deputies and four, equally, by the Senate; two are proposed by the government and two by the General Council of the Judiciary. The twelve members of the Constitutional Court of Belgium are nominated for life by the King, from a list of two names proposed alternatively, by a majority of two-thirds, by the Chamber of representatives and by the Senate. In Poland the fifteen members of the Constitutional Tribunal are elected for nine years by members of Parliament.

Generally, constitutional courts in Europe exercise an abstract review of statutes, independent of the factual circumstances of an individual application. Very often a case may be filed before such a court in two ways: by way of an application directed against the statute itself, typically at the instigation of political authorities; and, exceptionally, by way of a reference decided by one of the ordinary courts, before which the conformity of a statute with the constitution is at issue in the context of litigation. In this regard, the introduction in France of priority preliminary rulings on constitutionality brought the Conseil constitutionnel—having up until that point had jurisdiction only over cases brought before it anterior to the promulgation of the statute in issue—into line with Europe's other constitutional courts.

At times direct recourse to a constitutional court is open to an individual who claims that their fundamental rights have been breached. In Germany an individual may, after exhaustion of the remedies offered by the ordinary courts, bring a claim before the Federal Constitutional Court in connection with any legislative, administrative, or judicial act which 'individually, presently, and directly' violates their fundamental rights. In Spain the review procedure of *amparo* (the Spanish name for the remedy of protection of constitutional rights) allows individuals to bring a claim before the Constitutional Court in connection with any administrative or judicial act (but not a legislative one) which violates fundamental rights.

In this way a European model of constitutional courts is emerging. It is different from the American model of the Supreme Court. In Europe, constitutional justice is not dispensed by all courts, in all types of case, under the control in the final resort of the top court.

It is given to a specialized institution, distinct from the ordinary courts, composed of individuals chosen primarily by political authorities, and which, when a case is filed before it according to special procedures, has competence only in constitutional matters; but it is also the only institution competent to set aside laws as being contrary to constitutional rules or principles. Applying generally—*erga omnes*— the decisions of such a court apply to all, not only to those party to the proceeding before the court.

Quite apart from the existence of this concept of constitutional justice, the safeguarding of fundamental rights through the imposition of a duty to comply with fundamental principles even on primary legislation is an idea that is gaining traction in Europe. It confers greater authority on constitutional norms and it profoundly modifies the relationship between the courts and legislation. Even in the United Kingdom, the very byword for parliamentary sovereignty, the Appellate Committee of the House of Lords, replaced in 2009 by the Supreme Court of the United Kingdom as the court of last instance, took on the air of a constitutional court when it held, in *Belmarsh*,[11] that certain provisions of the Anti-Terrorism, Crime, and Security Act 2001 were in breach of the requirements of the European Convention on Human Rights underlain by the principles of habeas corpus of 1679 and the Bill of Rights of 1689.[12]

2. THE REINFORCEMENT OF JUDICIAL CONTROL WITH THE EXECUTIVE

The countries of Europe have followed a range of different courses when it comes to submitting public authorities to judicial review, in particular on the question of the unity or duality of the judicial order.

---

[11] *A v Secretary of State for the Home Department ('Belmarsh')* [2004] UKHL 56, [2005] 2 AC 68.
[12] See p 88 of this volume and R Clayton, 'The Belmarsh Case' in S Juss and M Sunkin (eds), *Landmark Judgments in Public Law* (Hart Publishing 2017) Ch 7.

The duality of judicial orders originated in the history of France. Its most ancient roots go back to the Conseil du Roi, as it began to emerge, with its counsellors of State (*conseillers d'État*) and counsel (*maîtres des requêtes*), from the reign of Philip IV of France (1285–1314), in the first period of the administrative monarchy. From the opposition between royal power and the *Parlements*—courts of law composed of the Nobles of the Robe, guardians of aristocratic privilege and liberty—arose the rule that the ordinary courts could not adjudicate on public affairs. In 1641 the Edict of St Germain-en-Laye expressly prohibited the ordinary courts from taking cognizance of cases 'concerning the State, administration or government which we reserve to ourselves alone and to our successor kings'. The Revolutionary law of 16 and 24 August 1790 took a similar line, providing that:

Judicial functions are distinct and will always remain separate from administrative functions. It shall be a criminal offence for the judges of the ordinary courts to interfere in any manner whatsoever with the operation of the administration, nor shall they call administrators to account before them in respect of the exercise of their official functions.[13]

The Decree of the Convention of 16 Fructidor An III (2 September 1795) confirmed this approach: 'The prohibition is renewed against the courts taking cognizance of the acts of the administration of whatever kind they may be.'[14]

Stretching back to the French Revolution and the Old Régime, the duality of judicial orders was consolidated by all subsequent regimes in France. The Consulate (the government by three consuls of the first French Republic 1799–1804) and the First French Empire (1804–14 and 1815) furnished this judicial architecture with its definitive character through the establishment of the Conseil d'État, by the

---

[13] See LN Brown and J Bell, *French Administrative Law* (5th edn, OUP 1998) 46.
[14] ibid.

Constitution of An VIII, and the Prefecture Councils, forerunners to the administrative tribunals, by the Law of 28 Pluviôse An VIII. All subsequent political regimes have upheld these institutions. When the Law of 24 May 1872, adopted at the urging most prominently of Gambetta, empowered the Conseil d'État to decide cases against the administration without the pretence that it was merely advising the head of state, administrative law was anchored in France; from then on the Conseil d'État had the acknowledged jurisdiction of a court.[15]

From this constitutional requirement the Conseil constitutionnel has in its case-law inferred two fundamental principles: first, the independence of the administrative courts;[16] and, secondly, the competence of the administrative courts, 'in conformity with the French conception of the separation of powers', to sit in cases concerning the annulment or the reversal of decisions taken by the executive in virtue of the prerogative.[17] With the constitutional revision of 23 July 2008, the duality of the judicial orders was inscribed into the Constitution itself. The Conseil constitutionnel has recognized the principle by emphasizing that the Conseil d'État and the Cour de cassation are 'the courts at the pinnacle of the two systems of law recognized by the Constitution'.[18]

The concepts resulting from this long history are entirely alien to the understanding of public law in the United Kingdom; indeed, at times these French concepts attract incomprehension and defiance across the Channel. '[T]he equal subjection of all classes to the ordinary law of the land administered by the ordinary Law Courts', was according to Dicey an important part of the English concept of the rule of law, which 'in this sense excludes the idea of any exemption of officials or others from the duty of obedience to the law which governs other citizens or from the jurisdiction of the ordinary tribunals'.[19]

---

[15] ibid 47.   [16] Decision No 80–119 of 22 July 1980.
[17] Decision No 86–224 of 23 January 1987 at [15]
[18] Decision No 2009–595 of 3 December 2009 at [3].
[19] JWF Allison (ed), *The Oxford Edition of Dicey Vol I* (OUP 2013) 233.

But, even if it is not as intimately linked to national history in other countries as it is in France, the duality of judicial orders is far from being a French exception in Europe. Within the European Union, in particular, it is rather the British model which seems exceptional. Other than the United Kingdom, one finds it only in Ireland, Denmark, Cyprus, and Malta. All other countries of the European Union have administrative courts, organized around the following three principal models.

First, many countries—Belgium, Greece, Italy, and the Netherlands—have in common with France a Council of State that exercises both consultative and judicial functions. In addition to the duality of judicial orders—the ordinary and the administrative courts—comes the Council of State's duality of functions, that is, judicial and consultative ones. Such a Council of State exercising two functions used to exist in Luxembourg too, until that country elected to create a supreme Administrative Court, which is distinct from the Council of State, the latter now exercising only the consultative function. Across different histories and traditions, the French model of the Conseil d'État has, therefore, not remained isolated.

In the Netherlands such a model goes back to the Empire of Charles V (1519–56) and received its modern form in 1814. Presided over by the King, it played an important role including, in the absence of a constitutional court, in respect of the application of the Constitution.

In Italy the Consiglio di Stato, created in 1831 for Piedmont–Sardinia, in 1861 became competent in respect of all Italy when Victor Emanuel II secured Italian unity. Since 1889 it has exercised both judicial and consultative functions which, in common with the Conseil d'État under the Third Republic, are optional in connection with draft legislation. A system of regional administrative tribunals, at the top of which the Consiglio di Stato sits, was created in 1971 and a Code of Administrative Justice was adopted in 2010.[20] Section 1

---

[20] Codice del processo amministrativo, 2 July 2010 (No 148/L).

of the code emphasizes the principle of the effectiveness of judicial review of the administration 'according to the principles of the Constitution and of European law'.

More recent is the Belgian Council of State. When the country was created, the Constitution of 1831 did not envisage a Council of State. The issue was debated from 1834 onwards; but it was not until the law of 23 December 1946 that a Council of State was put in place, with both consultative competences and judicial ones in respect of actions for annulment. A body of so-called auditeurs prepare the judgments, under the authority of the General Auditeur. A Council for Alien Law Litigation which, under the control of the Council of State, decides in cases related to the entry and stay of aliens, was furthermore created by a law of 15 September 2006.

In Germany adjudication in administrative law cases is carried out by an autonomous judicial system, which exercises only judicial functions, undertaking no administrative or consultative tasks. This organizational structure is a part of a context of judicial specialization, organized along five distinct systems, each of which has at its top a federal supreme court: the civil and criminal courts; the administrative courts; the financial courts, which sit in fiscal cases; the labour courts; and the social courts.

Without going quite so far in dividing up jurisdictional activities, many European countries have, in common with the German model, a system of administrative courts with exclusive competence. Austria, Bulgaria, the Czech Republic, Finland, Lithuania, Luxembourg, Poland, Portugal, and Sweden have adopted such a system. Some of these courts are ancient. Thus the Supreme Administrative Court of Poland, created originally by the Constitution of 17 March 1921, was reinstated by the Constitution of 2 April 1997; the voivodeship[21] administrative courts decide under its control. New legislation concerning

---

[21] A voivodeship is the highest level administrative subsivision in Poland; it corresponds to what in many other countries is termed 'province'.

administrative justice came on stream on 1 January 2004, just before Poland's entry into the European Union, on 1 May of the same year. Other courts are more recent, such as the supreme Administrative Court of Luxembourg which, on the heels of the *Procola* judgment of the European Court of Human Rights,[22] detached itself from the country's Council of State, now only consultative.

Thirdly, and finally, comes a group of countries where there is specialization only at the level of the supreme courts. This is, in particular, the case in Spain where, in addition to a Council of State that is only consultative, the administrative chamber of the Supreme Court sits in administrative law cases. Referred to as the third chamber—'*sala tercera*'—it exercises first-instance competences, especially in relation to measures taken by the Council of Ministers (in addition to its role of being the court of final instance). It has, in terms of its Supreme Court, complete autonomy. A similar model can be found in Estonia, Hungary, Romania, Latvia, and Slovakia.

Although the increasing complexity of the law and the interest of controlling the activity of the executive combine to encourage the separation of judicial orders, without however generalizing it, the strengthening of judicial review can be observed all over Europe. The UK example is particularly emblematic.

At the instigation most prominently of the Appellate Committee of the House of Lords, UK law has in the post-war period undergone considerable development in this connection.[23] When Parliament legislated by the Crown Proceedings Act 1947 to allow claims sounding in tort to be brought against the state, it abandoned the adage 'the King can do no wrong', which had meant that no petition of right lay for tort. In the wake of this development a law of state liability in tort has emerged.[24] As Sir Thomas Bingham MR observed in *X (Minors)*

---

[22] *Procola v Luxembourg* (1996) 22 EHRR 193.
[23] S Sedley, *Lions under the Throne: Essays on the History of English Public Law* (CUP 2015) Chs 6–14.
[24] See D Fairgrieve, *State Liability in Tort* (OUP 2003).

v Bedfordshire County Council, 'the rule of public policy which has first claim on the loyalty of the law [is] that wrongs should be remedied'.[25] From Lord Greene MR's judgment in *Associated Provincial Picture Houses Ltd v Wednesbury Corporation*,[26] the UK courts have developed their approach to judicial review, which allows the courts to review the legality of administrative decisions. Over time the three basic principles—legality, rationality, and procedural impropriety[27]— have been reinforced. Not only must an administrative decision be taken according to the requisite procedures: it must also not be 'unreasonable' or 'irrational'.[28]

Within the single judicial order, there is in the United Kingdom an increasing number of specialized bodies which sit in administrative law cases. Before the suit comes before a court, it is often obligatory to file a case before an administrative tribunal, an independent commission which will re-examine the case. These tribunals can most prominently be found within the fields of taxation, immigration, expropriation, and social benefits. The Tribunals, Courts and Enforcement Act 2007 gave them a common structure, by distinguishing first tier tribunals from upper tribunals. At the judicial level, an Administrative Court was instituted in 2000, within the High Court in London. Its judges are not specialists; but this court sits in all cases concerning public authorities.

Whatever the judicial organization opted for, the European countries have all increasingly opened up for judicial review of administrative decisions and tightened the courts' control of the activities of the administration. Amongst the many achievements of European public law is the requirement that a court should review that the administration acts in

---

[25] *X (Minors) v Bedfordshire County Council* [1995] 2 AC 633, 663. Also: *Jones v Kaney* [2011] UKSC 13, [2011] 2 AC 398 at [113] (Lord Dyson); *Michael and Others v The Chief Constable of South Wales Police and Another* [2015] UKSC 2, [2015] 1 AC 1732 at [186] (Lord Kerr).

[26] *Associated Provincial Picture Houses Ltd v Wednesbury Corporation* [1948] 1 KB 223, 233–4 (Lord Greene MR).

[27] *CCSU v Minister for the Civil Service* [1985] AC 374, 410 (Lord Diplock).

[28] That requirement of UK law implies that the decision must also not be disproportionate: P Craig, *Administrative Law* (8th edn, Sweet & Maxwell 2016) Ch 21.

accordance with the requisite procedures and take reasonable and proportionate decisions.

3. THE RIGHT TO AN EFFECTIVE REMEDY BEFORE AN INDEPENDENT AND IMPARTIAL TRIBUNAL

Access to Court

The principle of a right to an effective remedy before an independent and impartial tribunal is strongly emphasized in the Treaties of the European Union and the European Convention on Human Rights. In addition to Articles 6 and 13 of the European Convention comes Article 47 of the Charter of Fundamental Rights of the European Union, according to which: 'Everyone whose rights and freedoms guaranteed by the law of the Union are violated has the right to an effective remedy', which means access to an independent and impartial tribunal. Article 47 also provides that 'Everyone shall have the possibility of being advised, defended and represented' and that legal aid shall be available to those who lack sufficient resources in so far as such aid is necessary to ensure effective access to justice.

The European courts apply these provisions vigorously. For the European Court of Justice the right to an effective remedy—or the 'requirement of judicial control' as the Court put it in *Marguerite Johnston*—is a general principle of Community law.[29] By giving, on the basis of an extensive interpretation of the civil rights and obligations and criminal charges, a broad ambit to Article 6 of the Convention, the European Court of Human Rights is extremely vigilant both in regard to access to an independent and impartial tribunal[30] and the right to an effective remedy.[31]

---

[29] Case 222/84 *Marguerite Johnston* ECLI:EU:C:1986:206 [18].
[30] *Golder v United Kingdom* (1979–80) 1 EHRR 524, (1975) 57 ILR 200.
[31] *Kudla v Poland* (2002) 35 EHRR 11.

French administrative law has for a long time characterized as a general principle of law the right to a remedy to appeal any administrative decision as being ultra vires (*'recours pour excès de pouvoir'*)[32] and the right to appeal any judicial decision (*'pourvoi en cassation'*).[33] This case-law has received the imprimatur of the Conseil constitutionnel, which made the right to an effective remedy a constitutional principle.[34] European law has contributed to broadening the scope of this fundamental right. The subjection to judicial review of contracts entered into by the National Assembly in part stems from the requirements of Community law in the field of equality of access to public procurement,[35] whereas the opening up and then broadening of prisoners' access to court is largely, at least indirectly, due to the influence of the European Convention on Human Rights.[36] On that last point the Strasbourg Court vigilantly carries through its own principle that 'justice cannot stop at the prison gate.'[37]

The right to an effective remedy must be reconciled with the proper functioning of the courts. Especially as concerns the supreme courts, an excessively high number of appeals could compromise the exercise of their most fundamental function: that of ensuring the unity of the law and to decide new and important questions.

Most of the countries have limited the access to their supreme courts. In Europe, differently from in the United States, it is not a question of authorizing the supreme court to select for itself the cases which it will decide: in 2012 the US Supreme Court chose to decide seventy-three of the 7,500 appeals brought before it. But a system of permissions to appeal, which is traditional in the United Kingdom, is developing in Germany, Belgium, and Spain. Thus, among 5,173 individual applications filed

---

[32] Conseil d'État, 17 February 1950, *Ministre de l'agriculture c/ dame Lamotte.*

[33] Conseil d'État, 7 February 1947, *d'Aillières.*

[34] Decision No 86–217 of 18 September 1986; Decision No 88–248 of 17 January 1989.

[35] Conseil d'État, 5 March 1999, *Président de l'Assemblée nationale.*

[36] Conseil d'État, 17 February 1995, *Hardouin and Marie*; 14 December 2007, *Boussouar, Planchenault, Payet.*

[37] *Campbell and Fell v United Kingdom* (1985) 7 EHRR 165 at [69].

in 2013 with the Federal Constitutional Court in Karlsruhe, permission to appeal was granted in only 154 of them. A preliminary procedure has similarly been instituted before the Constitutional Court of Belgium. In Spain a 2007 statute drew up the framework of *amparo* and a 2011 one restricted the access to the Supreme Court, in particular in so far as concerned litigation of a pecuniary nature. Only 128 *amparo* applications were thus found to be receivable in 2012 out of more than 7,000 filed; nevertheless, the European Court of Human Rights has not found that these stringent requirements amount to a breach of the right of access to court.[38] In France a permission to appeal procedure was instituted before the Conseil d'État and the Cour de cassation when the 2008 reform set up a triage procedure for priority preliminary rulings on constitutionality by the Conseil d'État and the Cour de cassation. In Italy, however, whereas a procedure of '*rilevanza*' is in place before the Corte costituzionale, the access to the Consiglio di Stato and the Corte di cassazione remains extremely open, resulting in a worrying congestion of the two courts.

Fair Trial

The independence and impartiality of tribunals require increased vigilance. For the various Councils of State, there is no obstacle in principle to the exercise, by one institution, of both the consultative and judicial function; but it is necessary to make sure that one and the same person does not, exercising those two functions, examine one and the same question. The European Court of Human Rights made this point in connection with the Luxembourg Council of State, which at the time exercised both functions, by holding that a decision taken judicially by a bench of which four of five members had at an earlier time examined the same question within the context of their consultative function was a breach of the requirements of the Convention.[39]

---

[38] *Arribas Anton v Spain* (unreported) App No 16563/11 judgment 20 January 2015.
[39] *Proçola v Luxembourg* (1996) 22 EHRR 193.

Given the limited number of its members, the Luxembourg Council of State could scarcely organize itself differently and decided therefore to limit its role to the consultative function, the judicial function being accorded to an Administrative Court that is distinct from it. The situation is different in respect of the Councils of State that are able to take measures to ensure that a member does not examine the same question successively exercising the consultative function and then there judicial one. This is the case with the Dutch Council of State[40] and the French one.[41]

Necessary measures were taken in France by the Decrees of 6 March 2008 and 23 December 2011. By providing that 'the members of the Conseil d'État may not participate in giving judgment in cases directed against acts taken on advice of the Conseil d'État, if they have taken part in the deliberation of that advice', the Decree of 6 March 2008 reverts to the rule that had been enunciated, in very similar terms, by section 20 of the law of 24 May 1872,[42] before it was suspended, by reason of constraints connected to France's entry into the war, by the Decree of 4 October 1939, later repealed by the Decree of 18 December 1940. The Decree of 6 March 2008 furthermore modifies the composition of the benches giving judgment in the Conseil d'État better to secure the separation between the judicial section and the administrative ones. Given these precautionary measures, the European Court of Human Rights determined that the duality of functions of the French Conseil d'État was being exercised within a framework that complied with the requirements of a fair trial. The Decree of 23 December 2011 adds that members who examine a case at the preparatory stage and sit on the bench delivering the judgment shall not have access to the advice ('*avis*') and the dossiers produced

---

[40] *Kleyn v Netherlands* (2004) 38 EHRR 14.

[41] *Sacilor Lormines v France* (2012) 54 EHRR 34.

[42] Article 20 of the law of 24 May 1872: 'The members of the Conseil d'État may not participate in giving judgment in cases directed against decisions which have been prepared by the sections to which they belong, if they have assisted in the deliberation.'

by those members sitting in the consultative function regarding legislation at issue in the case.[43]

Even the most time-honoured traditions sometimes require revision, including those of the most highly esteemed legal systems, such as that of the United Kingdom. Thus the bailiff of Guernsey may no longer sit in the Royal Court of the Anglo-Norman island.[44] Perhaps less anecdotally, the Constitutional Reform Act 2005 substantially modified the organization of the court system of the United Kingdom, in a way that anticipated possible criticism which might have been made of it against the background of the requirements of a fair trial. The functions of Lord Chancellor, which used to include the participation of the officer-holder in all three branches of government—the legislative, the executive, and the judiciary—have been divided between three authorities: the Lord Chief Justice of England and Wales, an independent judge who sets out the directions of judicial policy; the Lord Chancellor, a member of Cabinet in charge of constitutional affairs and the appointment of judges; and the Lord Speaker, who presides over debates in the House of Lords. An independent commission—the Judicial Appointments Commission—made up of fifteen members selects candidates for judicial office; the candidates selected are then recommended to the appropriate authority (Lord Chancellor, Lord Chief Justice, or Senior President of Tribunals). The Supreme Court of the United Kingdom on 1 October 2009 succeeded the Appellate Committee of the House of Lords as the final appeals court. The members of the Appellate Committee became the initial twelve Justices of the Supreme Court. They remain members for life of the House of Lords; but they must abstain from participating in debates whilst they remain in judicial office, of which the retirement age has been set at seventy-five. The same rule will apply to their successors, if they are elected members of the House of Lords.

[43] See, generally, J Bell, *Judiciaries within Europe: A Comparative Review* (CUP 2010) 77–9.

[44] *McGonnell v United Kingdom* (2000) 30 EHRR 289.

Procedural rules develop in order properly to address the imperatives of a fair trial. These apply not only to courts but any institution which, by reason of its composition and powers, may be regarded as a tribunal in the sense of Article 6 of the Convention. That is the case with independent administrative authorities which, without being courts in terms of domestic law, have powers of sanction.[45] The public character of the hearings is now guaranteed in quarters where that used not to be the case, as in France before the judicial organs of professional associations[46] or before financial courts. The role of the reporting judge (*'rapporteur'*) in relation to the formation of the court has been redefined.[47] In the wake of the European Court of Human Rights' judgment in *Reinhardt and Slimane-Kaïd,*[48] the Cour de cassation substantially revised the rules applying to the Principal State Counsel's Office (which comprises Principal State Counsel and the Advocates General). Without the matter coming before any of the European Courts, the law of 16 February 2015 put a stop to the tradition in France of the Minister of Justice presiding over the Tribunal des Conflits, thus ending what might have looked like the last vestiges of the King's residual proper jurisdiction (*la justice retenue*).

An office peculiar to the French administrative court system,[49] the *Commissaire du gouvernement* exercised his or her duties in conditions which, although his or her independence was not questioned, attracted inquiries on the part of the European Court of Human Rights.[50] Even the title was a source of ambiguity. The decree of 7

---

[45] See eg Cour de cassation, 5 February 1999, *Oury;* 3 December 1999, *Didier and Leriche.*

[46] Conseil d'État, 14 February 1996, *Mableau.*

[47] *Didier v France* ECHR Reports of Judgments and Decisions 2002–VII p 433.

[48] *Reinhardt and Slimane-Kaïd v France* (1999) 28 EHRR 59.

[49] J Bell, 'The Role of the Commissaire du Gouvernement and the European Convention on Human Rights' (2003) 9 European Public Law 309; 'French Administrative Law and the Supremacy of European Laws' (2005) 11 European Public Law 487; ' "Interpretative Resistance" Faced with the Case-Law of the Strasbourg Court' (2008) 14 European Public Law 137.

[50] *Kress v France* ECHR Reports of Judgments and Decisions 2001–VI p 41; *Martinie v France* ECHR Reports of Judgments and Decisions 2006–VI p 87.

January 2009 changed the name to Rapporteur public and revised the procedure governing his or her activity: the gist of his or her conclusions are now available before the hearing; the parties may take the floor after having read the conclusions; and he or she does not assist in the deliberations before the administrative tribunals and the administrative courts of appeal, whereas before the Conseil d'État he or she is present unless a party demands that the Rapporteur public be recused. The Strasbourg Court has held that these new rules conform fully with the European requirements, emphasizing that— even on the admission of the Bar Council intervening in the case— the Rapporteur public contributed to the proper functioning of the adversarial process and the quality of justice.[51]

The requirement of disposing of proceedings within a reasonable time is taking on ever greater importance and a right to just satisfaction has developed in cases where that right has been breached. The right should be guaranteed at the domestic level.[52] As Italy has failed to develop a domestic procedure according to which breaches of this right are established and compensation is dispensed, numerous cases have been filed in this connection against this country, the contracting party where the domestic courts are the most congested with applications.[53] Present though not always explicit, the dialogue of judges manifests itself at three levels: between the European courts and the domestic courts; between the two European courts; and between the supreme courts of the various European countries.

'At the level of the European Community, there ought not to be government of judges, nor war of judges. There ought to be room for the dialogue of judges', declared *Commissaire du gouvernement*, as he

---

[51] *Marc-Antoine v France* (unreported) Admissibility Decision 4 June 2013 at [32]–[33]. Also: *Etienne v France* (unreported) App No 11396/08 Admissibility Decision 15 September 2009; *Escoffier v France* (unreported) App No 8615/08 Admissibility Decision 8 March 2011.

[52] See eg Conseil d'État, 28 June 2002, *Garde des sceaux c/ Magiera*.

[53] See eg *Bottazzi v Italy* ECHR Reports of Judgments and Decisions 1999–V p 15.

then was, Bruno Genevois in *Cohn-Bendit*.[54] The dialogue he urged has since become reality.

Within the framework of the European Union, this dialogue is organized and made possible by the preliminary ruling procedure. In this way close bonds have developed between the Court of Justice and domestic courts. From 1961—the year of the first preliminary ruling reference, made by a Dutch court—to 2014, 8,710 such questions have been asked of the Court. A large portion of the law of the European Union is created through such exchanges between courts. A total of 2,137 references have been made by the German courts, 1,279 by the Italian courts, 906 by the French courts (of which 110 made by the Cour de cassation; 93, by the Conseil d'État), and 573 by the UK courts. Incidentally the judgments of the Court of Justice handed down within this framework, in common with those that it hands down on the basis of direct applications, have the authority of *res judicata* in respect of all the courts of the European Union. The Conseil d'État has recognized their binding character, even when they go beyond the remit of the preliminary reference in the case at issue.[55]

The decisions of the European Court of Human Rights, however, have binding force only in respect of the particular cases that they settle and do not, from a strictly legal point of view, bind the other courts. But, although they are 'essentially declaratory',[56] they exert a strong persuasive effect, which give them the binding effect of interpretation. As the Court's then President, Jean-Paul Costa, observed in 2009:

> It is no longer acceptable that States fail to draw the consequences as early as possible of a judgment finding a violation by another State when the same problem exists in their own legal system. The

---

[54] Conseil d'État, 22 December 1978, *Ministre de l'intérieur c/ Cohn-Bendit*.
[55] Conseil d'État, 11 December 2006, *Société de Groot En Slot Allium Bv.*
[56] *Marckx v Belgium* (1979–80) 2 EHRR 330, (1979) 58 ILR 561 at [58].

binding effect of interpretation by the Court goes beyond *res judicata* in the strict sense.[57]

Everything thus depends on the extent to which domestic courts are prepared to listen and on the quality of the relations they maintain with the Strasbourg Court.

At times, however, the domestic courts betray a measure of reluctance. This is perhaps most clearly exemplified in the jurisprudence of the United Kingdom Supreme Court. Lord Phillips, then the President of the Court, observed in his judgment in *Horncastle* that although the requirement in the Human Rights 1998 to 'take into account' the Strasbourg jurisprudence will normally result in the Supreme Court applying principles that are clearly established by the Strasbourg Court, in certain cases the court may not do so, because the Strasbourg Court has not sufficiently appreciated or accommodated particular aspects of the domestic process.[58] The Supreme Court in *Horncastle* showed that it had the courage of its convictions, and it has in later cases stressed time and again that, although the domestic courts have the obligation to take into account the Strasbourg jurisprudence, they are not bound by it.[59]

In his judgment in *Osborn* Lord Reed explained that: 'The Convention cannot ... be treated as if it was Moses and the prophets. On the contrary, the European court has often referred to the "fundamentally subsidiary role of the Convention".'[60] But the Justices of the Supreme Court have been prepared to draw certain limits as to how far such an approach can be taken, especially when the Strasbourg Court has pronounced itself sitting as a Grand Chamber: 'there are

---

[57] Memorandum of the President of the European Court of Human Rights to the States with a View to Preparing the Interlaken Conference, 3 July 2009.

[58] *R v Horncastle and Others* [2009] UKSC 14, [2010] 2 AC 373 at [11] (Lord Phillips).

[59] *R (Osborn) v Parole Board* [2013] UKSC 61, [2014] AC 1115; *R (on the Application of Chester) v Secretary of State for Justice* [2013] UKSC 63, [2014] 1 AC 271; *Haney and Others v The Secretary of State for justice* [2014] UKSC 66, [2015] 1 AC 1344.

[60] *R (Osborn) v Parole Board* [2013] UKSC 61, [2014] AC 1115 at [56] (Lord Reed).

limits to this process, particularly when the matter has been already to a Grand Chamber once or, even more so, as in this case, twice, observed Lord Mance in his judgment in *Chester*.[61]

The Conseil d'État follows closely the case-law of the Strasbourg Court in connection with the effect of the latter's judgments within domestic law. Thus the Conseil d'État has held that the execution at the domestic level of a judgment of the Strasbourg Court necessitates that the government take measures both to repair the consequences that the violation of Convention rights has engendered and to remove the source of the violation.[62] But the domestic principle of *res judicata* stands in the way of the re-opening of a definitively closed judicial proceeding, at least when it is provided for by statute, as was the case with the law of 30 June 2000 in connection with penal procedures. Thus, in the absence of statute, neither the administrative courts[63] nor the financial courts[64] are to re-open a closed procedure after a judgment has been handed down by the Strasbourg Court. On the other hand, an administrative authority, such as the Financial Markets Authority ('*l'Autorité des marchés financiers*'), must re-examine a sanction.[65]

On less straightforward questions a dialogue may be entered into. The European Court of Human Rights has taken a strong line in connection with the principle *non bis in idem*, in particular in cases concerning the combination of an administrative sanction and a criminal penalty in respect of the same facts.[66] In a priority preliminary ruling of 18 March 2015 on constitutionality concerning insider trading,[67] the Conseil constitutionnel, without going quite as far as the European Court, developed its own approach. It decided that,

---

[61] *R (on the Application of Chester) v Secretary of State for Justice* [2013] UKSC 63, [2014] 1 AC 271 at [27] (Lord Mance).

[62] Conseil d'État, 4 October 2012, *Baumet*.

[63] Conseil d'État, 11 February 2004, *Mme Chevrol*.

[64] Conseil d'État, 4 October 2012, *Baumet*.

[65] Conseil d'État, 30 July 2014, *Vernes*.

[66] *Grande Stevens v Italy* (unreported) App No 18640/10 Judgment 4 March 2014.

[67] Decision No 2014–453/545 QPC and 2015–462 QPC of 18 March 2015.

if the insider dealing, punishable by criminal penalty, and insider misconduct, which can be investigated before the Financial Markets Authority, are of the same nature, a person may not, on the basis of the same facts, be prosecuted on both grounds.[68] No doubt the dialogue and jurisprudential adjustments on this sensitive question have only just begun.

For their part the two European courts listen, without doubt more and more, to the constitutional and supreme courts of the different States.

Obviously, tensions may at times arise. As regards the Court of Justice, the preliminary ruling mechanism and the integrated character of the legal order of the Union allow for tensions to be eliminated quickly. They may be more persistent in relation to the European Court of Human Rights. Four examples, concerning France, Italy, Germany, and the United Kingdom respectively, shed light both on the potential conflicts and the search for solutions to allay them, which includes the European Court reconsidering its case-law.

For the Conseil constitutionnel, the concept of 'judicial authority' comprises both magistrates on the bench ('*magistrats du siège*') and those exercising functions as public prosecutors ('*magistrats du parquet*');[69] indeed Section VIII of the French Constitution, entitled *On judicial authority*, specifically mentions public prosecutors ('*le parquet*').[70] In view of the ways in which they are nominated and the hierarchical authority that the Minister of Justice exercises over them, public prosecutors do not meet the standards of independence that the European Court of Human Rights requires of magistrates.[71] Nevertheless, in *Medvedyev v France* the Grand Chamber of

---

[68] ibid.

[69] Decision No 93–326 of 11 August 1993; Decision No 97–389 of 22 April 1997; Decision No 2010–14/22 QPC of 30 July 2010.

[70] See E Bjorge, 'The Vienna Rules on Treaty Interpretation Before Domestic Courts' (2015) 131 LQR 78, 98–100 on the confusion to which this can lead for common lawyers.

[71] *Moulin v France* (unreported) App No 37104/06 Judgment 23 November 2010.

the Strasbourg Court avoided clashing head-on with the case-law of the Conseil constitutionnel.[72] A planned constitutional reform giving magistrates serving as public prosecutors the same guarantees as those on the bench in respect of the ways in which they are nominated may no doubt reduce the scope of divergence. In addition, both the domestic courts and the European Court can go further in setting out which powers may be accorded to magistrates exercising functions as public prosecutors and which decisions need the intervention of a magistrate sitting as a judge.

In Italy a decree dating back to 1924[73] authorizes the presence of a crucifix in state schools. A number of cases had been filed on the subject; the Consiglio di Stato held that the crucifix may adorn the classroom walls, as a testimony, in a secular perspective—'*in un orizzonte laico*'—of the values of tolerance and respect for the human person irrespective of the religion professed by the pupils.[74] It may be noted that in Germany the Federal Constitutional Court took the opposite view, by holding that a Bavarian school regulation[75] authorizing crucifixes in state schools was contrary to religious liberty.[76] A very sensitive issue in Italy, the case was brought before the European Court of Human Rights in *Lautsi v Italy*. After an adverse Chamber judgment had held Italy to be in breach of Article 9 of the Convention, the Grand Chamber definitively upheld the decree and the Italian practice, determining that, given the absence of a European consensus on this question, the presence of crucifixes in classrooms fell within the States' margin of appreciation—but the States must nevertheless ensure that the choices made in this connection do not amount to a form of indoctrination.[77]

---

[72] *Medvedyev v France* (2010) 51 EHRR 39.

[73] *Ordinamento interno delle giunte e dei regi istituti di istruzione media* Decree No 965 of 30 April 1924, s 118 ('Each school must have the national flag and each classroom must have a crucifix and a portrait of the King.').

[74] Consiglio di State, 13 February 2006, Decision No 556.

[75] Schulordnung für die Volksschulen in Bayern, 21 June 1983 (GVBl. S. 597).

[76] BVerfGE 93, 1 *Kruzifix*.   [77] *Lautsi v Italy* (2012) 54 EHRR 3.

Whilst the Federal Constitutional Court at Karlsruhe had, in the name of freedom of expression, rejected the claim of Caroline of Monaco, the Princess of Hannover, against certain newspapers that had published photographs of her personal and family life,[78] the European Court of Human Rights in the same case condemned Germany for a breach of the right to family life.[79] The judgment of the European Court gave rise to acute tensions with the Karlsruhe Court.[80] But, in a second case, the Strasbourg Court dismissed the application based on the right to private life, by referring to the fact that, since the first case, German authorities had, by 'explicitly [taking] account of the Court's relevant case-law', thrown its support behind the approach set out by the Strasbourg Court, thus striking the correct balance between freedom of expression and the right to private life.[81] In a new case, concerning Prince Ernst August von Hannover himself, and not his spouse the Princess, the Court arrived at the same conclusion and, having emphasized the importance of the States' margin of appreciation, agreed with the judgment of the Karlsruhe Court, which had rejected the claim of breach of the right to private life.[82]

The most severe conflict between the European Court and a State concerns the question of prisoners voting in the United Kingdom. Legislation in the United Kingdom systematically takes away the right to vote from every prisoner. By its general and automatic nature, this disenfranchisement has, on numerous occasions, been held by the European Court to be disproportionate.[83] Without overruling its

---

[78] BVerfGE 101, 361.   [79] *Von Hannover v Germany* (2005) 40 EHRR 1.

[80] See HJ Papier, 'Das Bundesverfassungsgericht im Kräftefeld zwischen Karlsruhe, Luxemburg und Straßburg' in HP Hestermeyer and others (eds), *Coexistence, Cooperation and Solidarity Vol II* (Brill 2012).

[81] *Von Hannover v Germany* (2012) 55 EHRR 15 at [125]; *Axel Springer v Germany* (2012) 55 EHRR 6.

[82] *Ernst August von Hannover* (unreported) App No 53649/09 judgment 19 February 2015.

[83] *Hirst v United Kingdom* (2006) 42 EHRR 41; *Greens and MT v United Kingdom* (2011) 53 EHRR 21; *Firth v United Kingdom* (unreported) App No 47784/09 judgment 12 August 2014.

earlier case-law, the Grand Chamber of the Court may have nuanced it, finding no breach of the Convention in connection with Italian legislation which provided that criminal conviction meant disenfranchisement only in relation to sentences of three or more years and as a function of the prisoner's conduct and the gravity of the crime.[84] A restriction of prisoners' voting rights will not necessarily be automatic, general, and indiscriminate simply because it was not ordered by a judge; but such a restriction cannot apply generally and indiscriminately to any prisoner. In the United Kingdom the Supreme Court held in *Chester* that only Parliament could amend the current law.[85] At present, however, the House of Commons scarcely seems disposed to want to do so. The European Court of Human Rights therefore found a persistent violation of the Convention in a judgment against the United Kingdom concerning 1,015 prisoners, holding that the finding of a violation was equal to just satisfaction, such that no compensation was due to any of the applicants.[86]

More and more, the need arises also for the two European courts to co-operate with one another in the same spirit of dialogue. Gone are the days when their remits seemed entirely distinct: economic, customs-related, commercial, and fiscal law in respect of the Court of Justice; civil liberties and fundamental rights in respect of the European Court of Human Rights. The Court of Justice regards the guarantees of the European Convention on Human Rights as general principles of Community law and applies them taking into account the case-law of the Strasbourg Court. And, by adopting an extensive concept of the ambit of Convention rights, the Strasbourg Court often enters into the field of law covered by the European Union, especially in relation to the protection of property rights and the right to non-discrimination. It does so on the basis of the presumption

---

[84] *Scoppola v Italy* (2012) 56 EHRR.

[85] *R (on the Application of Chester) v Secretary of State for Justice* [2013] UKSC 63, [2014] 1 AC 271.

[86] *McHugh and Others v United Kingdom* (unreported) App No 51987/08 judgment 10 February 2015.

that secondary EU legislation respects the rights protected by the European Convention.[87] The Strasbourg Court has characterized a denial of a preliminary ruling from the Luxembourg Court as a breach of the right of access to court.[88]

With the Treaty of Lisbon, which confers on the Charter of Fundamental Rights the status of treaty and opens up the route to accession to the European Convention on Human Rights by the EU, the two courts—Luxembourg and Strasbourg—are called upon to engage in closer and closer co-operation. Having become used to the judicial dialogue that takes place between themselves and the two European courts, the constitutional and supreme courts of the different European countries strive for improved understanding between them, the better to be able to give coherent answers to the questions they are all facing.[89]

Whether it concerns the application of the law of the European Union or the interpretation of the European Convention on Human Rights, they are increasingly called upon to deal with the same issues. Quite apart from European law, they decide on the big societal questions that the different States encounter together, especially within the field of the role of public bodies in regulating economic and social relations, the relationship between the central State and the federal or devolved entities, the balance to be struck between security and liberty, the protection of the environment, and the preservation of sustainable development.

Thus the constitutional courts and the supreme courts of the European countries are closely associated with one another, through international partnerships that bring them together, increasingly regular bilateral meetings, and by establishing networks of exchange of information. Their decisions are ever more based on comparative law

---

[87] *Bosphorus Airways v Ireland* (2006) 42 EHRR 1.

[88] *Dhahbi v Italy* (ureported) App No 17120/09 judgment 8 April 2014.

[89] See T Bingham, *Widening Horizons: The Influence of Comparative Law and International Law on Domestic Law* (CUP 2010).

as between the European countries. In common with the universities, the courts have in Europe a decisive role to play in order that domestic law is more integrated with that of other European states.

Before the French administrative courts, the increasingly frequent references in the conclusions of Rapporteurs publics to the judgments of other European countries reveal the level of attention accorded to comparative law. In 2008 a Comparative law unit (*'Cellule de droit comparé'*) was created in the Conseil d'État, within the *Centre de recherches et de diffusion juridiques.*[90] It is not difficult to see evidence in the case-law of the working community that is emerging between the courts of the European countries. Perhaps an annual seminar— that for two or three days could bring together representatives of the Luxembourg and Strasbourg courts as well as all the constitutional and supreme courts of the countries of the European Union—might in the longer run reinforce the exchanges that growing interaction is making indispensable. Similar developments are affecting all public authorities.

---

[90] A Bretonneau, S Dahan, and D Fairgrieve, 'Comparative Legal Methodology of the Conseil d'État' in M Andenas and D Fairgrieve (eds), *Courts and Comparative Law* (OUP 2015) 242, 244.

6

A European Model of Public Administration

> I think it is safe to say that in the fourteenth century the various social, political, administrative, judicial, economical, and literary institutions of Europe were more nearly alike than they are now, though civilization has done so much to facilitate intercourse and efface national barriers.
>
> —Alexis de Tocqueville, *The Old Regime and the Revolution* (1856)

In accordance with its own history, every country defines the role of the State in its own way. Thus the role of the administration, the functions of the public apparatus, and its relations with civil society differ from State to State. This diversity is particularly evident in Europe. The European countries—their size and population varying greatly—have systems of public administration that address profoundly different requirements. In Europe nations are co-existing which, like France, over the course of a long history have structured themselves around the State; or like the United Kingdom or Spain, where the bureaucratic traditions are no less time-honoured but where the State has been of less importance in the collective life of the nation; and, finally, States whose foundations are more recent and uncertain. The Nordic and Scandinavian countries, based on the model of the welfare state, sit next to States which, having just left Communism behind, are turning to liberalism. Europe boasts unitary States, strongly decentralized States, and federal States. Neither

Towards a European Public Law. First Edition. Bernard Stirn. © Bernard Stirn 2017. Published 2017 by Oxford University Press.

the law of the European Union[1] nor that of the European Convention on Human Rights[2] privileges any particular type of administrative organization above others. EU law on the contrary is dedicated to the institutional and procedural autonomy of the Member States.

Nevertheless, certain common developments emerge, encouraging the diverse administrative systems more and more to co-operate with one another, indeed to link up in a network. These convergences, pointing up a European model of public administration, emerge on several fronts. They concern in particular the scope of public action, the ways in which the administration is organized, and the regime of the civil service.

1. THE SCOPE OF PUBLIC ACTION

Within the context of privatization, great public sectors have given way to a system where the relationship between the State and the economy is characterized by competition and regulation. Public authorities still have a duty, however, to ensure a level of solidarity in society, especially so far as concerns services of general interest.

Privatization, Competition, and Regulation

In the wake of the Second World War, vast public sectors developed in Europe, certainly in the countries under Communism, but equally in Western Europe, especially in France, the United Kingdom, Germany, and Italy. Throughout Europe States have since abandoned the idea of directly owning big industrial, financial, or banking enterprises; even transport, energy, and telecommunications companies have on the whole been privatized.

---

[1] Consolidated versions of the treaty on European Union and the Treaty on the Functioning of the European Union, [2016] OJ C202; Charter of Fundamental Rights of the European Union, [2016] OJ C202.

[2] Convention for the Protection of Human Rights and Fundamental Freedoms, 4 November 1950, 213 UNTS 221.

Initiated in the United Kingdom by the Thatcher government in 1979, the trend spread to Germany, Italy and, from 1986, France. There is a striking parallel between the privatization of British Telecom, British Airways, and British Rail in the United Kingdom; of Deutsche Telekom, Lufthansa, and the Postbank in Germany; and of telecommunications, the steel industry, and petrol in Italy. With the dismantling, from 1989, of the Soviet bloc, the countries of Eastern Europe, too, went from a collectivized economy to a regime of private enterprise in only a matter of years.

In France privatization began in 1986 and was suspended after François Mitterrand's re-election in 1988, Mitterand having advocated during the presidential campaign the theme of 'neither, nor'— '*ni, ni*'—neither nationalization, nor privatization. Since privatization was re-initiated in 1993, it has continued under successive governments. At the end of the process, the great banks (Société générale, Paribas, BNP, and Crédit lyonnais), industrial groups (Matra, Elf-Aquitaine, Péchiney, Saint-Gobain, Rhône-Poulenc, and Renault), as well as public utilities (Air France, France Télécom, Gaz de France) had been privatized. Companies such as RATP, SNFC, EDF (of which the state retains 84.5 per cent of the capital), la Poste, and Aéroports de Paris remain in public hands, however. A company is regarded as belonging to the public sector when half of its capital is held by public entities or by other public sector companies.[3]

The trend of privatization is not a necessary concomitant of the free market of the European Union. So far as EU law is concerned, it is up to each Member State to decide on the reach of its public sector and to define the ways in which it is organized.

The economic crisis furthermore led the States to acquire holdings in companies. In 2008 the British State thus acquired 57.9 per cent of the capital of the Royal Bank of Scotland in order to ensure the bank's

---

[3] Conseil d'État, 23 November 1978, *Defferre and Others*; Conseil constitutionnel, Decision No 83–162 of 20 July 1983.

survival. The same year a Strategic Investment Fund (*Fonds stratégique d'investissement*) was created in France which in 2012 was integrated in the new Public Investment Bank (*Banque publique d'investissement*), owned by the State and by the Deposits and Consignments Fund (*Caisse des dépôts et consignations*). Through its intermediary, the French State in 2014 acquired 14 per cent of the capital of PSA Peugeot Citroën, which was then experiencing great difficulties, on an equal basis with the Chinese car manufacturer Dongfeng. In 2015 the French State equally acquired 4.70 per cent of Renault's capital, taking its total participation of the company's capital up to 19.70 per cent. In the spring of 2015 it was getting ready to augment its participation in Air France by buying 1.70 per cent of the capital of which it already owned 15.88 per cent. These augmentations have principally had the aim of the government benefiting from the right to double-voting rights which the law of 29 March 2014 granted to any shareholders who held the same shares for at least two years, unless there is a vote to the contrary in the company's general meeting of shareholders.

There is, however, a relation between the imperatives of competition and the reduction of the number and the evolution of the nature of public enterprises. As they are incompatible with the requirements of the free market, public monopolies have over time disappeared, within the fields of transport, both by air and rail; energy; communication; telecommunications; and postal services. Before la Poste was transformed into a limited company, the fact that it was publicly owned gave it an implicit, unlimited guarantee on the part of the State, which amounted to state aid.[4] At all events, the law of the European Union necessitates the separation of regulator and operator: a company acting in the market cannot be in charge of regulating the same market.

More broadly, the single market follows the principles of free competition. From its beginnings, the Treaty of Rome[5] prohibited any

---

[4] Case C–559/12P *France v European Commission* ECLI:EU:C:2014:217.

[5] Treaty Establishing the European Economic Community, 25 March 1957, 298 UNTS 3, Art 85.

agreements, decisions, and concerted practices 'which have as their object or result the prevention, restriction or distortion of competition within the Common Market'. The European Commission has powers of investigation and sanction to fight cartels and abuse of dominant positions. Measures tantamount to state aid must be notified to the Commission, which may oppose them. It exercises control over concentrations between companies. In order to perform these different functions it works closely with domestic competition authorities, which can now be found in an increasing number of countries.

Quite apart from competition law, the intervention of States in economic life is done more and more through regulatory authorities, developed along similar lines in the various European countries and encouraged to work together at the European level. The French Financial Markets Authority (*Autorité des marchés financiers*), created by the law of 1 August 2003, is the equivalent to the Financial Services Authority in the United Kingdom and the Bafin in Germany. Communications and telecommunications regulators are everywhere being set up, two such authorities being in place in France, the *Conseil de supérieur de l'audiovisuel*, on the one hand, the *Autorité de régulation des postes et des communications électroniques*, on the other, whereas other countries often have one authority for both sectors. Regulation authorities have also been established in the field of energy (in France, the *Commission de régulation de l'énergie*) and transport (the *Autorité de régulation des activités ferroviaires*, which will become the *Autorité de régulation des activités ferroviaires et routières*). The economic crisis has only reinforced the role of public regulatory authorities, especially within the fields of banking, insurance, stock markets, and financial markets. The European Union has in these fields created its own bodies, the European Securities and Markets Authority, the European Banking Authority, and the European Insurance and Occupational Pensions Authority.

Solidarity and Services of General Interest

Although it promotes competition, the law of the European Union is increasingly coming to recognize the importance of services of general interest.

Already in the Treaty of Rome it was provided that the general rules of free competition apply to an '[u]ndertaking entrusted with the operation of services of general economic interest' only in so far as the application of such rules does not obstruct 'the performance, in law or in fact, of the particular tasks assigned to them'.[6]

Services of general economic interest thus defined largely correspond to the public services characterized in French law as industrial and commercial. The responsibility of organizing services of public administration remains the competence solely of the States, whether it concerns those broadly falling under the great offices of State (or '*services régaliens*' in France) defence, security, justice, and diplomacy, or services such as education, health, solidarity, and culture, which do not lend themselves to interventions in the market. As for industrial and commercial services, Community law has from the outset emphasized the principle of free competition, all the while taking into consideration the particularities of the tasks carried out by them.

Two complementary elements of this field of law appeared in 1992 with the Maastricht Treaty,[7] which underscored the importance of trans-European networks in the areas of transport, telecommunications, and energy infrastructures, affirming the importance of the objectives of the economic and social cohesion of the European Union. According to its Article 129b, 'the Community shall contribute to the establishment and development of trans-European networks in the areas of transport, telecommunications and energy infrastructures'; action by the Community shall aim at promoting 'the interconnection and inter-operability of national networks'. Special

---

[6] ibid Art 90.
[7] Treaty on European Union, 7 February 1992, 1757 UNTS 3, [1992] OJ C224/1.

attention is thus accorded to trans-European networks, which are indispensable to European exchanges and interaction. Article 130a of the Treaty for its part provides that the Community 'shall develop and pursue its actions leading to the strengthening of its economic and social cohesion'.

Another step was taken in the Treaty of Amsterdam,[8] which deals not only with services of general economic interest but also with services of general interest in the more general sense. Its Article 7D provides that 'given the place occupied by services of general economic interest in the shared values of the Union as well as their role in promoting social and territorial cohesion, the Community and the Member States ... shall take care that such services operate on the basis of principles and conditions which enable them to fulfil their missions'. Through these provisions, reiterated in Article 14 of the Lisbon Treaty,[9] EU law gives services of general interest the status of a 'shared value', at the heart of the Union's concern for cohesion and solidarity. The Lisbon Treaty furthermore has an Annex 9 on services of general interest.

From its decision in *Corbeau*,[10] concerning the Belgian postal service, and *Municipality of Almelo*,[11] concerning electricity services in the Netherlands, the Court of Justice has given full effect to the provisions of the Rome Treaty which allow for services of general economic interest to derogate from competition rules to the extent that that is necessary for the accomplishment of the particular tasks assigned to them.

Thus, according to *Corbeau*, it is permissible to offset less profitable sectors against profitable ones, with a view to ensure coverage of postal services of the whole territory. According to *Municipality of*

---

[8] Amending the TEU, the Treaties Establishing the European Communities and Certain Related Acts, [1997] OJ C340/1.

[9] Amending the Treaty on European Union and the Treaty Establishing the European Community, 13 December 2007, [2007] OJ C306/1.

[10] Case C–320/91 *Corbeau* ECLI:EU:C:1993:198.

[11] Case C–393/92 *Municipality of Almelo* ECLI:EU:C:1994:171.

Almelo restrictions on competition, such as guaranteed supplies, are allowed so long as they are 'necessary in order to enable the undertaking entrusted with such a task of general interest to perform it'.[12] The same reasoning led the Court to accept an importation monopoly then accorded to EDF and GDF in France.[13] It also led the Court in *Altmark* to circumscribe the boundaries of State aid, holding that financial compensation for the services provided by the recipient undertakings in order to discharge public service obligations did not have the character of state aid.[14] The Conseil d'État applied this case-law when it recognized the legality of the subventions accorded—in compensation for the burdens of public services undertaken—to the concessionaire in charge of the construction of the new airport Notre-Dame-des-Landes in Loire-Atlantique,[15] as well as to the operator of the ferries plying between Corsica and mainland France.[16] More generally, the Court of Justice leaves to domestic authorities a broad measure of discretion to define the ambit and the management of their public services.[17] Finally the Court ensures—in ways which are similar to the application in French law of the principle of equality in relation to the public service[18]—that everyone have a right of access to services of general interest without discrimination.

The European Commission has, in its work published as Green and White Papers, drawn up complementary perspectives which, in addition to services of general economic interest, concern all services of general interest. It published in the first instance communications, in 1996 and 2000, then a Green Paper on 21 May 2003 and a White Paper on 12 May 2004, on services of general interest in Europe.

---

[12] ibid [49].

[13] Case C–159/94 *Commission v France* ECLI:EU:C:1997:501.

[14] Case C–280/00 *Altmark* ECLI:EU:C:2003:415.

[15] Conseil d'État, 13 July 2012, *Communauté de communes d'Erdre et Gesvres et autres*.

[16] Conseil d'État, 13 July 2012, *Compagnie méridionale de navigation et autres*.

[17] Case C–179/90 *Merci convenzionali porto di Genova SpA v Siderurgica Gabrielli SpA* ECLI:EU:C:1991:464; Case C–163/96 *Silvano Rosa* ECLI:EU:C:1998:54.

[18] See eg Conseil d'État, 9 March 1951, *Société des concerts du conservatoire*.

A communication of 20 November 2007 concerns services of general interest. The Commission defines services of general interest generally as 'the services, both economic and non-economic, which the public authorities classify as being of general interest and subject to specific public service obligations'.[19] That is at the heart of the definition of a universal service, the provision of a defined minimum set of services to all end-users at an affordable price.

Thus concerns as to the provision of public services are increasingly present in EU law. Domestic conceptions of public services develop in parallel.

In the various countries of the EU, two factors have combined to change the face of public services. The first factor, which stems from the level of Community law, bears on the transposition into domestic law of the requirements of European law, in particular directives. The second, stemming from the domestic level, is connected with the dynamic, which varies as between countries but is present everywhere, that has at its origin the need for public services.

The transposition of EU law has reshaped domestic public services. This is the case particularly in countries, such as France, which have age-old traditions of public services. During the course of only a few years, telecommunications, electricity and gas, and the postal services have undergone profound transformations, putting an end to monopolies, opening up markets to competition, and reaffirming the obligations of public services. On a number of occasions the legislator intervened with a view to adopt far-reaching legislation which could, owing to the effect of European law, be adopted largely consensually. In relation to telecommunications, the law of 25 July 1996 organized the universal service and the law of 31 December 2003 defined the obligations of public services in this sector. As concerns energy, statutes were enacted entitled, revealingly, the law of 10 February 2000 relating to the modernization and development of the public utility

---

[19] COM(2007) 725 p 3–4.

of electricity, of 3 January 2003 relating to gas and electricity markets and public utility of energy, and of 9 August 2004 relating to public utilities of electricity and gas. In relation to postal services, after the adoption of the laws of 25 June 1999 and 20 May 2005, which began the process of opening the sector up to competition, the law of 9 February 2010 transposed into domestic law the Directive of 20 February 2008, thus transforming la Poste into a commercial public sector company. In fifteen years all of the companies that embodied the public service system *à la française* have changed entirely. France Télécom gave way to Orange; Gaz de France became GDF–Suez and then Engie. These companies continue to discharge functions of public service, with the requirements that follow. Thus the governing bodies of EDF may, with reference to the continued delivery of public services, regulate the right to strike in those nuclear power plants whose contribution to the supply of electricity is indispensable.[20] But the framework within which they operate and are managed has been profoundly remodelled in order to respond to the requirements of European law.

In connection with public utilities, every country has its history peculiar to it and its needs. Differences have been striking between the different European countries in that regard. In the wake of the war of 1870 there was a real schism between, on the one hand, the German *Rechtsstaat*, 'a State governed by the rule of law',[21] founded on law rather than on state action and, on the other, the Republican values of the French public service then emerging. Today the Anglo-Saxon model, generally held to be more liberal, can be contrasted with the rather higher level of interventionism of the Latin countries. Beyond these differences—and although the challenges of public services differ from country to country—the need for public utilities appears to be felt all over Europe.

---

[20] Conseil d'État, 12 April 2013, *Fédération Force Ouvrière Energie et Mines*.
[21] See *Consistency of Certain Danzig Legislative Decrees with the Constitution of the Free City*, PCIJ Series A/B No 65, 1935, p 54.

Key public services are under constant pressure; in particular the need for security and the demand for justice are everywhere on the increase. Social cohesion more and more depend on the provision of public services. The economic and financial crisis has led to a growing interest in regulation and at times the intervention of the State. The same goes for the fears arising in connection with major public health risks. The great stakes of the protection of the environment and sustainable development, too, call for public policy.

Although European law is developing the public service of the various European countries, it has in this way also, on the whole, opened up for the public services new and broader vistas.

2. THE WAYS IN WHICH THE ADMINISTRATION IS ORGANIZED

The modalities of administrative action are in several respects changing. In the face of economic and budgetary difficulties, there is an ongoing search for shared principles and better governance. Delegated management is developing; procurement is having to abide by stricter requirements and more competition than before. Independent authorities and agencies play an ever more important role. More broadly, the principle of good administration is asserting itself.

Shared Principles and Better Economic Governance

Whilst monetary policy is largely entrusted to the European Central Bank, the budgetary policy of the States is carried out in an increasingly European framework. Within the network of European central banks, the European Central Bank conducts the monetary policy of the Union; for the nineteen Euro countries, it heads the Eurosystem. The decision announced in September 2012 by its president, Mario Draghi, to refinance the debt of the Eurozone members by making purchases—so-called outright monetary transactions—in secondary sovereign bond markets comes close to putting it on a par with the great central banks such as the Federal Reserve and the Bank of England. The wish to avoid another crisis has reinforced its powers. It thus controls all the financial establishments—banks, insurance, financial markets—and has a European Systemic Risk Board.

In budgetary terms, the Stability and Growth Pact, adopted on 17 June 1997, by the Amsterdam European Council,[22] and implemented by the Regulation of 7 July 1997, set a deficit limit of 3 per cent of GDP and set the public debt to GDP ratio at 60 per cent. If excessive deficits did occur, the Council could draw up recommendations, issue formal notices, and as a final resort impose sanctions on the State at issue.

Although this framework was relaxed in 2005, it became impossible to respect it due to the economic crisis a few years later. But it contributed to tighten solidarity within the Eurozone and to take into consideration the need for greater rigour in the management of public finances.

Referred to as the six pack, as it consists of five regulations and one directive, a stability and growth pact was adopted in October 2011. In addition to these EU measures, the countries of the Eurozone in May 2010 added the creation of the European Financial Stability Facility, which on 1 July 2012 became the European Stability Mechanism, an international financial institution with a capital of €700 million, aiming to face up to the challenges encountered by the Eurozone countries in the management of their sovereign debt. It is authorized to give loans of up to €500 million.

An intergovernmental agreement, the Treaty on Stability, Coordination and Governance in the Economic and Monetary Union,[23] known as the European Fiscal Compact, was signed on 2 March 2012

---

[22] Resolution of the European Council on the Stability and Growth Pact, 17 June 1997, [1997] OJ C236.

[23] Treaty on Stability, Coordination and Governance in the Economic and Monetary Union, 2 March 2012, not published in the Official Journal.

by twenty-five States Members of the European Union, the United Kingdom and the Czech Republic having elected not to associate themselves with it.

This treaty draws up demanding obligations within the field of public deficit and debt, with the mid-term objective of no structural deficits above 0.5 per cent of the gross domestic product, or 1 per cent for those states whose public debt is below 60 per cent of the gross domestic product. It aims for greater co-ordination of economic policy and better governance of the Eurozone. By adopting this golden rule, it provides that the State shall introduce in their legislation measures guaranteeing the balance of public accounts, either 'through provisions of binding force and permanent character, preferably constitutional', or through provisions which, as is the case with the legislation put in place in France, are fully respected and adhered to 'throughout the national budgetary processes'.[24] In case of excessive public debt, the Member State in question shall reduce it at an average rate of one-twentieth per year.[25] The Treaty confers on the Court of Justice the power to decide on alleged breaches of its provisions and, if need be, to impose on the peccant State a lump sum or a penalty appropriate in the circumstances, not exceeding 0.1 per cent of its gross domestic product.[26]

In an original fashion, the Treaty provides that it will enter into force, in respect of those States which ratify it, after its ratification by twelve States whose currency is the euro and then, in respect of other States, as they ratify it.[27] It entered into force on 1 January 2013. Within five years, at most, the States shall ensure that the Treaty is incorporated into the legal framework of the European Union.[28]

The Treaty has been approved along the parliamentary route, Ireland being the one country to have organized a referendum, which, in May 2012, gave a positive result (60 per cent 'yes', with a participation rate of 50 per cent). In no country did the Treaty encounter

---

[24] ibid Art 3(2).   [25] ibid Art 4.   [26] ibid Art 8(1)–(2).
[27] ibid Art 14(2)–(3).   [28] ibid Art 16.

constitutional difficulties. Thus, by its decision of 9 August 2012, the Conseil constitutionnel held that the Treaty reinforced obligations already provided for within the legal framework of the European Union, without breaching the essential conditions of the exercise of sovereignty; it could therefore be ratified by France without there being a need for constitutional revisions.[29] Similarly the German Federal Constitutional Court held, on 12 September 2012, that the Treaty was not contrary to the Basic Law.[30] Its conformity with EU law was recognized by the *Pringle* judgment of the European Court of Justice on 27 November 2012.[31]

National budgetary procedures were adopted as a consequence of the Treaty. Thus, in France, the *loi organique* of 17 December 2002 relating to the programming and governance of public finances was implemented by the High Council of Public Finance, which is presided over by the First President of the Cour des comptes, and organizes the dialogue with the European Commission during the course of the domestic budgetary process.

Acting again within the framework of the European Union, the European Council meeting at Brussels on 29 June 2012 added a 'growth pact' to the various measures. This pact, which had been initiated by President François Hollande, allows for €120 billion. It takes the form of a declaration included in the statement of conclusions of the European Council. With a view to contributing to its application, a European Fund for Strategic Investments was created in 2015.

With these variegated developments between the workings of the institutions of the European Union, the measures taken within the framework of the Eurozone and intergovernmental decisions, the pursuit of a common governance—within the budgetary and fiscal fields especially—is more and more emerging as a real prospect.

---

[29] Decision No 2012–653 of 9 August 2012. [30] BVerfGE 132, 195.
[31] Case C–370/12 *Pringle* ECLI:EU:C:2012:675.

Delegated Management and Public Procurement

With a view to managing the provision of services, there is a desire for more efficacy, flexibility, and involvement of the private sector. In that regard, the French model of concessions is an historic example.[32] It is spreading today under the more general sobriquet of delegated management. Experiences are mutually enriching each other through exchanges between the countries: the UK private finance initiative (PFI) has directly inspired the French public private partnership (PPP). In these two countries, the risks to which the process may lead, notably for local authorities, have given rise to greater regulation. Within the field of public procurement, the European framework requires transparency, publicity, and competition.

Directives, recast by three directives of 26 February 2014, which must be transposed within two years, set procurement rules applicable in all public works, services and supplies, as well as service concessions, determining rules peculiar to the so-called particular procurement regimes of energy, water supplies, transport, and postal services.

Ensuring competition, transparency is required of all the actors within the field of public procurement. All public tenders above specific contract values must be published. The contract value thresholds above which an invitation to tender must be published are €5,225,000 for public works and, for service and supplies contracts, €135,000 for the State and €210,000 for public authorities. Above those thresholds a minimum procedure is required, guaranteeing a 'degree of advertising sufficient to enable the services market to be opened up to competition and the impartiality of the procedures to be reviewed'.[33] It is incumbent on the States to put in place effective remedies in order to ensure respect for the obligations of sufficient advertising and

---

[32] See eg Conseil d'État, 11 March 1910, *Compagnie générale française des tramways* (conclusions: Blum); the *Commissaire du gouvernement*'s conclusions are reported in (1910) 17 Revue du droit public 274.

[33] Case C–324/98 *Telaustria* ECLI:EU:C:2000:669 at [62].

competition. This is why French law has developed the so-called pre-contractual interim relief procedure, which makes it possible to bring a case before contracting, and thereafter the contractual interim relief.

In a way that transcends domestic categories, EU law applies in this field to all 'contracting authorities'. This category covers any body, whatever its nature under domestic law, that has legal personality, is established for the specific purpose of meeting needs in the general interest, and is under the effective control of public authorities.

The criteria on which the choice is made must be set out. They concern the price and the quality of the service as well as the capacity of the candidate to meet the needs of the public authority. They may include a range of concerns, notably social[34] or environmental ones.[35]

Basing itself on an approach which could already be found in the case-law of domestic courts, notably that of the Conseil d'État,[36] the Court of Justice has recognized that public authorities may themselves render the services that they need, without having to turn to the market and this without having to put in place the procedures of advertising and competition. In-house contracts can in other words be awarded without the need for an invitation to tender, between a local authority and an entity over which the former exercises control similar to that which it exercises over its own services.[37]

Independent Authorities and Agencies

The Swedish Ombudsman—appearing for the first time in 1713 and having been written into the Constitution of 1809—is indubitably the first independent administrative authority created in Europe, indeed in the world. The idea behind the office was to confer on one independent person the task of receiving and processing complaints on the part

---

[34] Case 31/87 *Beentjes* ECLI:EU:C:1988:422.
[35] Case C–513/99 *Concordia Bus Finland* ECLI:EU:C:2002:495.
[36] Conseil d'État, 29 April 1970, *Société Unipain*.
[37] Case C–107/98 *Teckal Srl* ECLI:EU:C:1999:562; Case C–159/11 *Azienda Sanitaria Locale di Lecce, Università del Salento* ECLI: EU:C:2012:817.

of citizens against the administration. At first the idea spread to the countries of Northern Europe—Finland in 1919, Denmark in 1955, and Norway in 1962. In 1967 the United Kingdom adopted the same approach, giving the office the title the Parliamentary Commissioner for Administration.[38] Within a few years the idea had become so widespread that it covered all the European countries and the majority of the States of the world. The French equivalent, the *Médiateur*, instituted by the law of 3 January 1973, became by virtue of the law of 13 January 1989 the *Médiateur de la République*. Taking inspiration from the office of the Defender of the people which had been put in place in Spain in 1982, the constitutional revision in France on 23 July 2008 created the *Défenseur des droits*, which by reason of the *loi organique* of 29 March 2011 brought under one umbrella the *Médiateur de la République* as well as the three other offices charged with the protection of rights.[39] At the European level, the European Ombudsman, created by the Maastricht Treaty, receives and examines complaints directed at the EU institutions.

Whatever the name—ombudsman, *médiateur*, *défenseur des droits*—the functions fulfilled are largely the same. It is an independent institution that is easily accessible for citizens in relation to any question regarding the relations of public bodies and citizens. In addition to the requirements of legality guaranteed by the courts, the role of the ombudsman is to ensure the correct handling of files, to guarantee that they are dealt with fairly, and to propose, when the need arises, reforms if legislation and applicable procedures need changing.

Following the Swedish example, the different European countries have developed independent authorities within the domain of the relations between the administration and citizens. Such authorities have also appeared, in rather a different area, as an appropriate way of improving market regulation. The role that these bodies have come to

---

[38] Parliamentary Commissioner Act 1967.
[39] The three were the *Défenseur des enfants*, the *Haute autorité de lutte contre les discriminations et pour l'égalité* and the *Commission nationale de déontologie de la sécurité*.

play in the administrative organization in Europe stands as an example of common developments.

A similar development can be observed in relation to the role conferred on agencies, which are given the task of carrying out, with considerable autonomy in relation to their management, operational action within a determined area, all the while playing a structuring role with regard to the area. In common with the development of the ombudsman, the development of this institution, too, was pioneered by Sweden, whose 1809 Constitution created agencies. The agency model is widely relied on in the United States, and was adopted in the United Kingdom, where it came to make up one of the axes of the administrative reform instituted following *The Next Steps* report of 1988.[40] The administration in the United Kingdom counts more the 120 agencies. Other European countries—Italy, Germany, and Spain in particular—have followed suit; the same goes for France where, through a number of legal constructs, agencies have, in numerous fields, become enforcers of public policy. The focus of the 2012 report of the Conseil d'État was on agencies, the report's title being 'Agencies: A New Form of Public Management?'[41]

At the European level some forty agencies have been created, over which the Commission exercises varying levels of authority.

The Principle of Good Administration

The Court of Justice has in its case-law progressively developed obligations on the part of the institutions and organs of the European Union in their relationship with citizens.[42] Files must be seriously examined, individually and concretely, respecting the requirements of impartiality. The principle of proper administration is recognized

---

[40] K Jenkins, K Caines, and A Jackson, *Improving Management in Government: The Next Steps* (HMSO 1988).

[41] Conseil d'État, *Les agences: une nouvelle gestion publique?* (Conseil d'État 2012).

[42] See P Craig, *EU Administrative Law* (2nd edn, OUP 2012).

as being part of the general principles of EU law.[43] In 2000 the Commission adopted a Code of Good Administrative Behaviour for relations with the public.[44] It provides that Commission staff must be objective and impartial and emphasizes the principles of legality, non-discrimination, and proportionality.

On the heels of these initial developments, Article 41 of the Charter of Fundamental Rights codified the '[r]ight to good administration', which it defines as the right of any person to 'have his or her affairs handled impartially, fairly and within a reasonable time by the institutions and bodies of the Union.'[45]

Three guarantees flow from this right. Every person has the right to be heard, before any individual measure which would affect him or her adversely is taken.[46] Every person has the right to have access to his or her file, while respecting the legitimate interests of confidentiality and of professional and business secrecy.[47] Finally, the administration has an obligation to give reasons for its decisions.[48]

Article 41 recognizes that every person possesses the right to have the Community make good any damage caused by its institutions or by its servants, 'in accordance with the general principles common to the laws of the Member States'.[49] It guarantees that every person may write to the institutions of the Union in one of the languages of the Treaties and must have an answer in the same language.[50]

As the Charter proclaims, good administration is focused on the relations between the administration and citizens. It concerns less the overall organization and effectiveness of the services than rights held individually by the citizenry vis-à-vis the services. In the treatment of the files submitted to it, the administration of the European Union has obligations of diligence and impartiality. Rights generally recognized by domestic law as belonging to the citizenry have been

---

[43] Case C–255/90P *Burban* ECLI:EU:C:1992:153.   [44] [2000] OJ L267.
[45] Charter of Fundamental Rights of the European Union, [2010] OJ C83/389, Art 41(1).
[46] ibid Art 41(2).   [47] ibid.   [48] ibid.
[49] ibid Art 41(3).   [50] ibid Art 41(4).

transposed to the level of the European Union, especially within the fields of the rights of the defence, access to administrative documents, reasoned decisions, and the liability of public authorities. The great convergence of rights recognized in these varied fields by the Member States has facilitated the development of the rules applicable to the European Union.

3. EUROPE AND THE CIVIL SERVICE

An aspect and an expression of State sovereignty, the civil service seems at first glance scarcely to have any connection with the European project. But, in common with the other means of action of public authorities, it swiftly underwent developments inspired both by Community law and the European Convention on Human Rights. Whilst they exhibit great differences in this regard, the various systems of permanent professional branches of state administration have therefore undergone developments which are common to them all.

The European Union has its own civil service. Its rules furthermore have a bearing on the civil services of the States Members.

Within a framework peculiar to it, the European Union employs approximately 56,000 civil servants, in the service of the general Community interest.[51] A regulation of 29 February 1968 gave the Community civil service its status,[52] which has later been reformed time and again, most recently in a regulation of 22 October 2013, which came on stream 1 January 2014.[53] The Civil Service Tribunal

---

[51] 38,000 for the Commission, 7,659 for the Parliament, 3,500 for the Council, and 2,100 for the Court of Justice.

[52] Regulation No 259/68 of the Council of 29 February 1968 laying down the Staff Regulations of Officials and the Conditions of Employment of Other Servants of the European Communities and instituting special measures temporarily applicable to officials of the Commission, [1968] OJ 56/1.

[53] Regulation No 1023/2013 of the European Parliament and of the Council of 22 October 2013 amending the Staff Regulations of Officials of the European Union and the Conditions of Employment of Other Servants of the European Union [2013] OJ L287/15.

was instituted in order to hear cases concerning disputes between the European Union and its civil servants.

While the public administration seemed to be excluded from the free movement instituted by the Rome Treaty, the Court of Justice brought the civil service within the ambit of Community law through its landmark decision of 17 December 1980, *Commission v Belgium*,[54] according to which free movement applies to all workers, with the sole exception of those who are, directly or indirectly, entrusted with the exercise of powers conferred by public law and with responsibility for safeguarding the general interests of the State. There is thus a distinction between positions in which the holder wields a portion of the State's sovereign power, positions in which the holder is not covered by the law of the Union, and other employees of the civil service, who are more numerous, to whom the entirety of rules flowing from the requirements of Community law apply.

Important consequences follow from this. With the exception of employment where the office holder wields a portion of the State's sovereign power, the citizens of the European Union enjoy access to the entirety of public employment in the different Member States. In France the law of 26 July 1991, and above all the law of 26 July 2005, lifted the statutory obstacles which (with some rare exceptions, such as higher education) until then made French nationality a condition for those wishing to become civil servants. In order to gauge the qualities of candidates, diplomas and professional experience must be mutually recognized and, although a 'concours', a competitive examination, is not in itself an obstacle to freedom of movement, it cannot be imposed on citizens of the European Union who are already qualified in their own country: a Portuguese hospital director may exercise his functions in a French hospital, without having to pass the examination of the *École nationale de la santé publique*, if the director had received in Portugal equivalent training to that which the French school offers.[55]

---

[54] Case 149/79 *Commission v Belgium* ECLI:EU:C:1982:195.
[55] Case C-285/01 *Burbaud* ECLI:EU:C:2003:432; Conseil d'État, 16 March 2005, *Ministre de la santé c/ Mme Burbaud*.

As applied in the law of the European Union, the principle of equality implies strengthened requirements within the law governing the civil service, from the point of view especially of the equality between the sexes. Recruitment must be equally open to men and women, with the sole exception, which will be rigorously policed, of the requirements peculiar to certain kinds of employment. Men and women have the right to the same benefits, notably as regards pensions.[56] Provisional arrangements are, however, acceptable.[57]

The European Convention on Human Rights, too, is concerned with the civil service. In the first place, the European Court of Human Rights, drawing on the case-law of the Court of Justice in connection with employment where the office holder wields a portion of the State's sovereignty, excluded these office holders from the ambit of Article 6 of the Convention.[58] It later modified its case-law, by deciding that there will 'be a presumption that Article 6 applies' in all ordinary labour law conflicts concerning civil servants; only cases concerning the 'special bond of trust and loyalty' which exists between a civil servant and the State are excepted.[59]

In common with freedom of association, the freedom of opinion and freedom of speech of civil servants finds support in the Convention. These rights and liberties on the one hand and obligations of reserve and neutrality on the other are combined within the strict proportionality inquiry to be undertaken.[60] Thus the Court has held that it was disproportionate to remove a German teacher from her position on the basis of her membership in the Communist party;[61] similarly, it

---

[56] Case C–366/99 *Griesmar* ECLI:EU:C:2001:648; Conseil d'État, 29 July 2002, *Griesmar*.

[57] Conseil d'État, 27 March 2015, *Quintanel*.

[58] *Pellegrin v France* (2001) 31 EHRR 26.

[59] *Eskelinen v Finland* (2007) 45 EHRR 43 at [62]. Also: *Blandeau v France* (unreported) App No 9090/06 judgment 10 July 2008.

[60] See p 110–15 of this volume.   [61] *Vogt v Germany* (1996) 21 EHRR 205.

judged it to be a breach of the Convention that no trade unions were allowed in the French army.[62]

In the teeth of the convergences stemming from the law of the European Union and the law of the European Convention, the national civil services differ from one another in a great many ways; that is a consequence of national history, on the part both of the State and of the decentralized authorities in public employ, and on the reach of the ambit of the concept of the 'civil servant'. In the United Kingdom the Civil Service counts only a limited number— approximately 550,000—of employees within its central services. Recruited on the basis of application and interviews, these members are subject to strict political neutrality: they must resign if they wish to run for Parliament and for the European Parliament. In Germany the great majority of the members of the public service belong to the *Länder* and only 40 per cent of the officials of the federal State are civil servants, *Beamte*; the rest are governed by the ordinary rules of labour law.

Similar reforms have, nevertheless, been adopted. The most notable ones were undertaken in Italy and in Spain. In Italy the laws of 1997 and 1999 put an end to the recruitment of civil servants by public law contracts; provided, at the director-level, aptitude lists as well as nominations for limited periods of time; and developed the concept of merit based remuneration. In Spain the law of 12 April 2007 simplified the categories of civil servant; opened up a greater space for contractual workers; provided for evaluation and remuneration on the basis of merit; and encouraged mobility. In both countries the reduction of the number of civil servants is noticeable. Similar developments can be seen in France, at the same time as the professional code of ethics and the concern to avoid interests of conflict are becoming more established. Here, too, developments common to the

---

[62] *Matelly v France* (unreported) App No 10609/10 judgment 2 October 2014.

European countries can be observed: the number of civil servants is being brought under control, if not diminished; contracts are being relied on more and more; merit plays an increasingly greater role in connection both with remuneration and promotion; mobility is increased; and, finally, concerns connected with the professional code of ethics and conflicts of interest are more and more pronounced. As for the civil service of the European Union, the Regulation of 22 October 2013 is in line with this development.

7

Conclusion

I love the past but I envy the future.
—Ernst Renan, *Recollections of my Youth* (1883)

The movement is afoot. By means of three circles—the law of the European Union, the law of the European Convention on Human Rights, and domestic law—a European public law is emerging. European public law is one of the foundations of the European edifice as a whole; it is also dependent on the larger whole, on its uncertainties, its hesitations, its delays.

Although the road travelled over the course of sixty years opens up broad vistas, predictable obstacles have made them less than certain. 'Gods would be needed to give laws to men', wrote Rousseau.[1] Without demanding as much of European public law, it is up to the citizens, to the courts, to the States, to the European institutions to ensure that this common project will be a lasting one.

In order to strengthen, European public law needs, in common with the rest of the European project, in the first place the support of Europe's citizens. Though they were pioneers in European integration, the French are not above succumbing to withdrawal, especially during difficult times. 'One has the tragic sentiment that the opening

---

[1] JJ Rousseau, *On the Social Contract* (tr JR Masters, St Martin's 1978 [1762]) 68.

Towards a European Public Law. First Edition. Bernard Stirn. © Bernard Stirn 2017. Published 2017 by Oxford University Press.

up of Europe and the world has led in France to intellectual provin-
cialization and withdrawal into Frenchness', wrote Pierre Nora.[2]

The British, having become associated with the common enterprise
only at a later stage, have their hesitations and at times aspirations
towards a return to insular isolation. Whilst the prospect of Brexit
is evoked, the referendum promised by David Cameron, victor in
the elections of May 2015, has given rise to anxiety. In Greece, the
government formed in January 2015 by Alex Tsipras, following the
victory of his party, Syriza, in the legislative elections, maintains complex relations with the European Union, against a backdrop where its
debt crisis has not been entirely overcome. More generally, economic
difficulties have meant that a schism between Northern Europe,
active and effective, and Southern Europe, spendthrift and poor has
emerged. In the East the new democracies, having just consolidated
their independence, at times show reticence to commonly applicable
rules. But, whatever their country of origin, the citizens of Europe
know, too, that they share a cultural heritage and partake of the same
economic and social whole, of which the values are the foundations
of the future.

Within the European area, the courts are learning to fulfil their
functions by referring to one another. For a function closely connected with sovereignty, such a multipolar approach is not a matter
of course. It is making itself felt, however, by means of the authority
of the two European courts, of reciprocal judicial dialogue between
domestic supreme and constitutional courts, of an emerging network
of judges. The quality and the unity of European public law depend
directly on the capacity of the courts to accomplish together that
common undertaking, which constitutes one of the foundations of
the shared European project.

For the States, joining the European project by giving up sovereignty is a challenge which can be met only with the conviction that

---

[2] P Nora, 'Préface' in S Barluet (ed), *Édition de sciences humaines et sociales* (Presses universitaires de France 2004) 9.

a greater framework than the national one is necessary in order to exercise one's sovereignty properly. Between inter-State relations and supranational competences, a fragile and uncertain equilibrium demands of the States constant adjustments. In the unique configuration that is the European Union—sharing the characteristics both of the confederation and of the federation—the States embody nations. Masters of the Treaties,[3] the States remain the prime movers. But they know that they cannot exist fully without tightening their relations and working more closely together.

It is for the European institutions to know how to exercise their role all the while respecting the domestic authorities, to ensure the continued trust of the citizens of Europe, and to instil greater confidence. Although they are inspired by the democratic ideal, they do not yet embody it to the degree they must, in spite of the undeniable progress of the election of the European Parliament by universal suffrage and the broadening of its powers, as well as the institution of the office of a permanent president of the European Council. Given that there is no structured political life at the European level, Europe suffers from a democratic deficit which leads to the search for means to furnish it with greater legitimacy.

For all—whether citizens, judges, States, shared institutions—law is assuredly one of the keys to the political project which is the continuation of the European project. Built from its first beginnings on law, Europe has brought about a legal evolution, all the stronger for the fact that—supported by the two important vectors of EU law and the European Convention—it has been able to draw on the resources of domestic law. Without any doubt one must look to the creation of the United States to find a similar renewal of legal categories. Transcending the distinction between the common and the civil law, European law, and especially European public law, appears already as a new model, ready to take its place among the great legal systems.

---

[3] BVerfGE 89, 155 at 190.

The European ambition goes beyond Europe. Already in 1968 Louis Armand wrote that 'Europe is no longer Europe but only a part of the world'.[4] In the time of globalization the remark is more germane than ever before. Like its economy, Europe is not isolated from the world. It partakes of the greater whole of public international law, all the while enriching that body of law. As there exists no system that is as organized and as structured beyond the State, European law is renewing the way in which international and domestic law co-exist, the way in which the State and the law co-exist. A transatlantic trade and investment partnership may be negotiated between the United States and the European Union. Within the broader frameworks established at the level of the United Nations, Europe is playing a role in adding force to the great conventions and covenants on the protection of refugees,[5] civil and political rights,[6] economic and social rights,[7] the rights of the child,[8] the global organization of trade,[9] the protection of biodiversity,[10] the fight against climate change,[11] and sustainable development.[12] By becoming stronger and stronger, European public law is opening up vistas which—like the genius of Europe—exceed the European continent.

[4] L Armand, *Le Pari européen* (Fayard 1968) 19 ('*L'Europe n'est plus l'Europe mais seulement un morceau du monde*').

[5] Convention relating to the Status of Refugees, 28 July 1951, 189 UNTS 150.

[6] International Covenant on Civil and Political Rights, 16 December 1966, 999 UNTS 171.

[7] International Covenant on Economic, Social, and Cultural Rights, 16 December 1966, 993 UNTS 3.

[8] International Convention on the Rights of the Child, 20 November 1989, 1577 UNTS 3.

[9] Agreement Establishing the World Trade Organization, 15 April 1994, 1867 UNTS 187.

[10] Convention on Biological Diversity, 5 June 1992, 1760 UNTS 79.

[11] Framework Convention on Climate Change, 5 June 1992, 1760 UNTS 79.

[12] Declaration on Environment and Development, 12 August 1992, A/CONF.151/26 (Vol 1), Annex I.

Index

Index